Honey, Do These Earrings Make Me Look Fat?

Real Life. Real Love. Real Laughs

DIANE PASCOE

ISBN 13: 9798743793730

Library of Congress Control Number: 2021908632

CONTENTS

INTRODUCTION

My tenth-grade English composition exam began when the teacher handed out a list of twenty topics and we had to choose one on which to write. I quickly saw a topic for me: My Most Embarrassing Moment.

A week later, the teacher came into the classroom carrying a stack of compositions that she plopped on her desk. "I would like to read a very funny story," she said, smiling. She was barely one sentence into the essay when I realized it was mine. It was the best moment ever.

It took another 40 years before I started writing my personal humour essays in earnest. After our move to North Carolina, I was unemployed for over a year, but when the corporate voices were silenced, I heard my own voice and began writing about my life. Even after I started working again, I continued to write until I retired, when my first two books were published: *Life Isn't Perfect but My Lipstick Is*, and *Never Argue with a Wiener Dog: You'll Lose*.

In this collection of essays, I have written about moments in my own life, as well as my life with my husband, known in my essays as "Honey" or my "Love God." He is patient and tolerant of my periodic urge to lose weight, which is more than any woman can ask.

My humor is typically self-deprecating, directed at me and my flaws but there are many supporting characters in my life who have added much fun, such as my sisters, my mom and my friends. I'm grateful that they are such good-natured women.

Humour propels my books, but I also share the lessons I have learned as I reflect on life when it has gone sideways. My goal when I write is to lift people up and lighten their loads. I hope I have achieved that.

THE TRIUMPH OF HOPE OVER EXPERIENCE

The party is over.

The bathroom scale has been merciless, and my clothes seem to have shrunk. Mirrors tell me I'm fat, except for my favourite magic mirror which makes me look long, thin and lovely for reasons that escape me.

I know from experience that if I want to change my eating habits, I need to track my weight and the calories I eat, so I signed up for a free weight tracking app. But here's the bummer— I'm supposed to weigh myself every day—I even get love notes from the app telling me what a good girl I've been when I weigh myself daily.

But I don't always like weighing myself every day. When I'm gaining weight, I weigh myself every year or two, and it takes a 10-pound gain to get my attention— then I have a cookie to feel better. I only like weighing myself daily when I'm losing weight. If the scale shows an increase of even a tenth of a pound, the wind almost goes out of my sails. But I refuse to give up.

Last week was the first time I had weighed myself in many months. I leaned to the left on the scale hoping it would give me a smaller number, then I leaned to the right in case that worked better. I got off the scale, then got back on, weighing myself a second time. Hmmm, a pound lower. I weighed myself a third time, which yielded a weight in between the first two. A fourth desperate weigh-in ten minutes later was the highest weight yet.

That did it! My scale was unreliable and indecisive, so it had to go. I jumped in the car and hightailed it to the department store to find a dependable one.

Once in the store, I waddled around many departments—the pharmacy, house appliances, beauty supplies, and the bathroom section—but no scales. But it wasn't all bad news — I figured I had lost at least four ounces walking around that megastore twice so this search was not a complete waste of time.

I finally asked the pharmacist where the scales were, and she told me to go to—are you ready? —the hardware department! Yup, the scales were with the toilet seats, lamp fixtures, and toilet plungers. I stared at shelves of scales, then settled on a scale whose package promised accuracy and reliability.

When I got home, I shed all my clothes, then got back on my old scale a few times out of curiosity. Once again, that thing flashed three different weights. Feeling optimistic, I boldly hopped on my new scale. It flashed a weight that was a pound less than my lowest weight on the old scale. Hallelujah! I weighed what I thought I should after a week of eating like a hummingbird. I couldn't wait to tell Honey about it.

"How do you know which scale is wrong?" he asked, Stirring the proverbial pot, he continued, "Maybe the new one is untrustworthy too. Maybe you need to have four or five scales—you can weigh yourself on each one then take the average of all your weights."

Gosh! Maybe he's right—five scales ought to work well. I can set up a spread sheet on my laptop that automatically averages my daily weights on all five scales. That will be the weight I report on my weight loss application. But this won't be a cheap solution because we will need to build a bathroom addition for more floor space for the three additional scales I will need to buy.

But we all know that I will simply go with the lowest weight of the five scales. Choosing the lowest weight will help me feel good about myself so I can carry on with my weight loss mission. I refuse to give up or give in. Hope always triumphs over experience.

Now be honest—do my earrings make me look fat?

TOGETHERNESS

If I must be hunkered down with another human being during this pandemic, I'm with the right guy.

Honey is smart, handsome, funny, a great cook, a good kisser, and a fast puzzle-doer. Best of all, he doesn't mind if I watch all my favourite murder shows, as long as he can watch some news shows, and the fishing show. Oh yeah, and the show about the vet, plus any shows about cars. And of course, all golf and hockey shows too. OK, football in the fall.

But I don't want to create the impression that life in our house is perfect. It isn't. With all this togetherness, we do have moments when we are out of sync, out of touch and out of nice words. One of us might make a snarky comment, or maybe we don't even speak for a time. But we have poor memories, so we soon can't remember why we aren't talking, and the silence ends as quickly as it began.

It's not only Honey and I who are experiencing the challenge of togetherness as we follow our county's stay-at-home rules. Honey said the internet reported that the

Royal Canadian Mounted Police in Canada said it had zero reports of home burglaries, traffic accidents, or vehicle break-ins, and 42,931 reported fights between couples in a twenty-four-hour period.

Even a conversation about this report caused a little cuffuffle with Honey:

Me: "What was that number of fights again?"
He: "42,931"
Me: "And who did they say it was between?"
He: "I just told you (eyes bulging)!"
Me: "Yeah, but I was typing it — you were talking too fast, and I couldn't remember the exact wording. Tell me again, ok?"

And here are a few more themes of our conversations if you can call them that:

On communication:
He: "I can't read your mind Di. You have to be clear."
Me: "I was extremely clear, but either you weren't listening, or your ears don't work. You know very well what I meant."

On technical matters:
Me: "Can you show me how to get that thing back on my laptop screen, please?
He: "Jeepers, Diane! I have shown you how to do it at least ten times!"

Me: "I know you have, but I still don't understand what you mean. Please.... explain it just one more time."

He: "Fine. But you'll need to find yourself a new Network Support Manager. This one's going on vacation."

On delicate matters:

Me: "How did you sleep last night, Honey?"

He: "Not that well. It was kind of noisy in the bedroom."

Me: "Huh? Are you saying I was snoring?"

He: "Got to go on my walk now. Bye!"

On word pronunciations:

Me: "That's not how you pronounce that word, Honey."

He: Well, just how do you think it's pronounced?"

Me: "Like this_____" (I pronounce it correctly.)

He: "This is like living with the grammar police."

Me: "Just trying to be helpful."

Some moments are worse than others, of course. One night I was having a very fitful sleep, mentally juggling my to-do list for the next morning. At 4:30 am, our wiener dog started scratching at our bedroom door. Honey got up with the dog and went to the living room. I rolled over, entering phase two of my sleep—no husband, no dog, no light, no noise.

Suddenly at 6:00 am, I sat upright in the bed when I heard a rooster crowing. "Cock-a-doodle-doo! Cock-a-doodle-doo!" Where did that noise come from? I wondered. Then the light came on, so to speak.

Honey had selected this sound as his tablet's wake-up alarm, except he wasn't in bed to wake up—I was. I crawled across the bed and hit all the buttons on the tablet screen, desperate to shut it off. Nothing worked, so I charged into the living room, his tablet clutched in my hand. That annoying man was watching the news and enjoying a cup of coffee.

The tablet was still crowing as I advanced towards him, undecided whether I would throw it at him or hand it to him. Civility prevailed and I handed the cock-a-doodle-doo-ing contraption to him.

"This was my only morning to sleep late. How do you shut the darn thing off?"

Calmly he said, "Look, you just press this button. See, its easy. Now, go back to bed."

Yeah, sure. I'm wide awake, scared silly by a rooster wannabe.

But like our other clashes, this also passed, and the rooster wake-up call became a joke between us later—well, OK, much, much later. Laughter is the glue that binds us together through good and bad, thick, and thin.

By the way, he now has a soft Caribbean melody as his tablet alarm.

Smart move, Honey.

LET IT GO

My mom and I have kept our bond strong in this last stage of her life through regular phone calls and trips back home to visit her. At least we did before the pandemic hit.

A number of years ago when I was planning to fly to Canada to see Mom, we had a good phone chat about my visit. She was looking forward to seeing me, she said, and she agreed that it was too bad my husband couldn't come with me on this trip.

A few days later I flew from Wilmington, NC to Detroit, MI, then drove two hours from Detroit to London, ON where Mom lived. When I opened the door to her house, Mom was genuinely surprised to see me, although I had called her only an hour before I arrived when I stopped for gas.

"I'm so happy to see you!" she said. "I didn't know you were coming here! Where's your handsome husband?." Whoa! I instantly realized that she didn't remember our conversations at all. *But I also decided that it just didn't matter. I let it go.*

We had a wonderful visit that day, laughing and talking about my childhood, Dad, and our old neighbours.

"When did Dad die?" she asked me during our chat.

"In 2012," I answered. Time flies when you're a ninety-one-year-old widow, so I know it's hard to remember the dates of many events, no matter how significant they are.

Over the next hour, she asked me eight more times when Dad died. Eight more times I answered, "2012." *It didn't matter if she asked her question nine or ninety times. I let it go.*

Mom can forget what she is going to do within minutes of agreeing to do it, and she often tells fibs just to end a conversation she doesn't like. The morning after I arrived, I asked her, "Have you had breakfast, Mom?"

"Yes," she lied. She doesn't like eating breakfast so it's easier to just say "yes" to throw the questioner off her trail. *But it just didn't matter—whatever worked for her. I let it go.*

My sister, Janet, arrived at Mom's later that afternoon to join us for dinner at The Little Beaver Restaurant, which I think is a good Canadian name, eh?

"Mom, it's time for a shower," Janet said. Like many seniors, having a shower is low on her list of things she wants to do.

"Ok, I'll have one now," Mom said. She disappeared into her bedroom, then reappeared ten minutes later, dressed to go out.

"Did you have your shower, Mom?"

"Oh, yes."

When Mom sat down on the sofa, Janet went into her bathroom. The shower was as dry as the desert. *It didn't matter. She'd have a shower tomorrow. We let it go.*

While eating dinner at the restaurant, Mom was reminiscing about the death of the family wiener dog, Heidi, thirty years earlier.

"I remember when Dad told me that Heidi had died under the coffee table during the night," she told us, as she had so many times before. "But when I went downstairs to see her, she woke up, walked over to me, and put her head on my foot, as she always loved to do. Then she died again." *It didn't matter how many times she thought the dog died. We let it go.*

Mom likes her memories just as she wants to remember them, even if they are fictitious. *If her version of life doesn't hurt her or anyone else, I can just let it go.*

There were also some very lucid moments in my conversations with Mom. Her views on world events and people were thoughtful and wise, often amazing me. And I learned that she could still solve problems when presented with a challenge like the one I described to her shortly before leaving for Detroit.

"Honey loves Shreddies cereal," I told her, "but we can't buy Shreddies in the US. I wish I could take him a box of cereal but unfortunately it won't fit in my suitcase."

As she sat on the sofa wrapped in her plaid throw blanket, she suddenly brightened up. "I know what you can do. You can pour the cereal into your suitcase and it will fill up all the empty spaces around your clothes!"

I was taken aback by her out-of-the-cereal-box thinking and proud of her for being so creative, although I ultimately decided that I didn't want Shreddies crumbs nestled in all my clothes.

Mom's contentedness and joy with her simple life on the sofa watching TV is reassuring. But her memory is getting worse by the day, and we must pay attention to issues she doesn't discuss, such as the wounds on her legs where she has banged them, or dental issues.

For those of us lucky enough to still have our parents, it isn't about their stories being factually correct; it's about their being happy. They can tell their stories any way they want to at this stage of their lives. There's only so much time left with our parents so there's no point in wasting it arguing about things that don't matter. What really matters is that the balance of their lives should be as rich and meaningful as possible.

RECLAIMING THE LOVE NEST

I am fed up, frustrated and infuriated.

Our wiener dog, Carley, has managed to work her way into our bed every night since Wyatt the Lab died a year ago. She lost her friend and since then we have felt sorry for her. However, she soon believed it was her *right* to sleep with the big people, and we have never told her otherwise. Who could blame her for thinking she had the same status as Honey and I? I am not *part* of the problem—I am the *whole* problem.

The wiener is going to return to sleeping in her dog bed in the living room and it isn't negotiable, but I'm afraid to tell her as she doesn't handle change well.

Why now? It's simple. Honey and I have not been sleeping well with her in our bed—we toss and turn every time the doxie diva moves, farts or snores. She burrows under the sheets in the centre of our king size bed, most often lying horizontally, while we hang on the edges of the mattress to give her room.

Her little black spikey hairs cover the sheets and cling to our faces. I suspect that her hairs have even been sucked into our lungs. I admit I have considered buying her pajamas to capture those little hairs.

Since she joined us in our marital bed, we have had to plan our love life carefully. When we're in the mood for lovin', we sneak into the bedroom, shutting the door quickly before she can charge into the room. She scratches at the door, whining and whimpering with her ear to the door, while we hug, kiss and coochie coo. When we're done, we bring her back into the bed so we can have peace and quiet. Then Honey and I wave goodnight to each other as we roll over to our respective mattress edges to give her highness some space.

No more. Her Royal Shortness needs to learn that Honey and I are the bosses, and she is going to go back to sleeping in her dachshund cave. We told her we were done with her sausage sleepovers in our bed. She just stared at us, suddenly pretending to understand only German.

The first night was hell. I took her outside to pee, then put her in her cave bed about 10 PM. Honey and I then headed into our bedroom, shut the door tightly and jumped into our bed. The crying, whining and door scratching began. I yelled "Carley go to bed!" which she did for five minutes. Then Honey also yelled at her to go to bed. She was quiet for an hour, then she started her whimpering again. This routine went on until 2:30 AM when I finally left the love nest for the sofa where she slept with me until breakfast. Yeah, yeah— I know, but I really needed some sleep.

The second night we made progress—less crying, less door scratching. We slept more and woke up feeling great, until the other shoe dropped. We found a pile of revenge in the dining room which was her way of telling us, "Poop on you guys —this new sleeping arrangement sucks."

The third night was the turnaround. There wasn't much fussing from the diva—we only had to yell at her twice. The three of us slept through the night in our respective beds until 5:00 AM. It had been such a good night. Or at least I thought it had been, until once again I found a pile of poop exactly where she had pooped the night before.

One night at a time, Honey and I have reclaimed our love nest. We take three wiener steps forward, two wiener steps back, but at least there's no crying, no whimpering, no scratching. We just need to work on a plan to stop her periodic revenge. It's always something with a wiener dog.

I learned an important lesson from this experience: never start doing something a dog likes if you aren't prepared to continue it forever. Dogs don't let go easily. Just like people.

WOMEN BE WARNED

I'm starting to look like a dalmatian.

Age spots have popped up everywhere, so I decided that it was time to have a dermatologist take a peek to be sure that the spots aren't dangerous. At 69, with years of basking in the sun, you never know if skin cancer is lurking behind a spot.

I also needed her to look at the rosacea rash that blossoms on my face making me look like a wrinkly-faced woman fighting teenage acne. Life stress has brought the bumpy rash back after twenty years of absence. When does it end?

Soon after I arrived at the dermatologist's office, I was hustled into an examination room where the assistant asked me to remove all my clothes and put on a robe. Hmm, usually I leave my white cotton granny panties on during my skin checks, but no problem.

The dermatologist soon entered the room. We had never met before so we exchanged pleasantries, maybe even smiles, although who could tell under our masks. Then, out of nowhere, she asked an unexpected question. "Are you comfortable with me examining your genitals at the end of our session?"

Whoa! The other shoe just dropped.

No dermatologist has ever asked me if they could check down there. In the past, dermatologists have checked my back, my front, under my arms, between my toes, all over my scalp but never my hoo-haw. Maybe the doctor had a double major in medical school and graduated as a derma-gynecologist.

But not wanting to seem like a prude, I agreed to the full Monty. Afterall, there's skin down there too.

Then I started to worry. If I'd known that someone would be looking closely at my hoo-haw or bum-bum, I would have polished and fluffed things up a bit before my appointment, just to be sure there were no stray bits of cheap, one-ply toilet paper hiding. Oh well, too late now.

The derma-gynecologist had a plan: we'd first do my frontside, then my backside, freezing any little skin blemishes and bumps that didn't belong there. Then she would inspect my hoo-haw and bum-bum—my words, not hers— at the end of the exam.

The skin examination began. She checked all the visible skin on my frontside, moving the gown around as she worked so that I could keep some measure of modesty. She lifted this, probed that, looked at my scalp under my grey hair then studied my neck, ears, elbows, and hands. All was fine on my frontside, she said.

I rolled over onto my stomach, much the way a walrus sunning on a rock would roll over. She checked the skin on my backside from my heels to my hairline, including a cheek-spread view of my bottom. Good heavens!

Then it was time for her to check my front private bits, so I did one more walrus-roll onto my back. She poked around my hoo-haw, then looked up and asked her assistant to make a note that I should return in three months. She said she wanted to recheck an area that she said, "lacked pigment." I could only picture Michael Jackson's face. She wasn't saying much, and I was saying even less, so we left it at that.

But by the time I got home, curiosity was getting the best of me. I tried to peek at my private bits with my little mirror but even with one leg up on a chair, I couldn't see much under the poor bathroom lighting. The light outside on the front porch would be so much better, I thought, but... nah.

Instead, I turned on all the lights in the bedroom, lay down on the bed, opened the room-darkening shutters and got my large round magnifying mirror to really see what was going on. But it was hard to position the mirror to see what she saw, as my arms are short, and my tummy is big.

OK. I have a Plan B. I will ask Honey to take a quick peek to see if he can see something unusual. Nah-uh. I'm certain he'd keep his eyes shut anyway.

Between this medical mystery, Covid-19, hurricanes, and the western wildfires, I am a nervous wreck. I guess

I'll have to wait until my next appointment to understand this hoo-haw thing. Maybe she will say that I need to expose my bits to some sunshine. I'm game for anything. Life was so much easier when I had dermatologists who weren't interested in my nether region.

Women be warned. This is not your mother's skin check anymore.

EAGLE EYE

My husband is an observant man. He's been this way since we met thirty-three years ago, and likely long before that too. Maybe it's his experience as a microbiologist that makes him notice the trivial things that others don't. Or maybe it's because he's a Virgo.

Early in our marriage, I decided that the little ball-shaped brass finial on top of the lamp in the living room was boring, so I found a small pineapple-shaped brass finial at the local lighting store. No big deal. I replaced the finial while he was at the hockey arena, but when he walked in the house, and before he had even said hello, his eyes locked on the new finial.

"Is that a new thingy on top of the lamp?" No other man would ever notice that there is a thingy on the lamp, let alone comment on a new one.

"How would you ever notice that little thingy?" I asked.

"I'm observant," he said. *That's an understatement, Honey,* I whispered under my breath.

He also notices what I wear. One afternoon I wore a new long grey sweatshirt that I had just bought that morning. Not beautiful. Not something anyone would turn their head to look at. I walked into the living room, sat down on the sofa, and waited for the comment. Nothing. Then we chatted about the weather and the news. I went back into the bedroom to get my glasses then reappeared in the living room. Still nothing. *Maybe his superpowers are waning.*

Then as I got up to go to the kitchen, it happened.

"Is that a new sweatshirt?" he asked. Bingo! I responded with my usual answer as if we were in a well-practiced marital dance.

"This old thing? Jeepers, I've had it for, umm…. 2 hours." I smile, he smiles. It is what it is. I never lie.

Yesterday I accidentally wore two different earrings – a pearl stud and a silver stud. Thankfully, he noticed this mistake with his eagle eye, and then let me know that my ears didn't match.

He also notices if I wear a new lipstick colour—even the Pantone people wouldn't be able to distinguish it from my other 327 lipsticks.

Sometimes I even appear in clothes that I have owned for a while but never worn, and can thus respond in good conscience, "Oh this old thing? I've had it for months."

I couldn't hide anything from him, even if I wanted to. This week I bought a new flannelette nightgown to prepare for cool nights in the love nest. He noticed it hanging on the hook in our bedroom.

"I see you have a new negligee," he commented, tongue-in-cheek. I could tell that I was more excited about my new sleepwear than he was.

Even my new purple shampoo that is supposed to make my battleship grey hair more silver hasn't escaped his attention in the shower stall where it hides behind six shampoos that promise thicker, cleaner, or silkier hair.

"Why would anyone want purple hair?" he mused to me post-shower. I didn't bother trying to explain how it works, but it does.

He always notices new decorative sofa cushions, tea towels, and brands of peanut butter that would escape the scrutiny of most men. But for a man who is very observant, it's odd that he doesn't seem to notice dust bunnies, a kitchen counter covered in crumbs or a bathroom mirror dotted in toothpaste splatter. Nah-uh, it is more likely that he does notice and doesn't give a hoot.

There is something warmly reassuring about Honey's attentiveness, and if he weren't so observant, I'm sure I'd wish that he were.

I love him just the way he is, eagle eye and all.

THE DAY I WAS FIRED

I'm going to be flat-out honest with you. I was fired once from a position I had always wanted. It was the supreme failure of my life to that point. I had no one else to blame, though goodness knows I tried. With this firing I entered the Hall of Shame, where you get to ponder your failures for the rest of your life.

Being fired hasn't been my only failure, of course. Being divorced also suggests loser behaviour, but I jointly own that one with my ex-husband, Mr. Wrong, and as you'd probably guess, I believe he owns the bigger share of the blame. Well, that's my story, and I'm sticking to it.

When I first got the f-word from the boss, I was stunned. I was fired in front of my peers. I sobbed. It was my dream job because it possessed fame, glory, and prestige. I loved the position, though in retrospect, I was wholly unprepared for the responsibility, the technical requirements, and the spotlight it put me in.

I remember f-day like it was yesterday. I can vividly recall that my brown hair was cut in a bob, with crooked bangs sloping from left to right. I could imagine what the neighbours said: *Lordy, did that girl get her hair cut by the hairdresser or the dog groomer?* Even I, a four-year-old, knew I looked weird.

Yup—I was four years old when I was fired.

The nightmare happened when I was in the kindergarten rhythm band. I was usually relegated to banging two sticks together or clanging the triangle. I didn't like playing the sticks...it was like putting Baby in the corner. I wanted to be the lone glorious drum pounder or the tambourine shaker, not a crummy twig tapper.

Then one day my teacher, Miss Koyle, asked me if I'd like to be the band conductor. You know, like Ricky Ricardo or Mitch Miller. My flat chest puffed up; my shoulders went back. I was handed the baton, led up to the platform, and turned around to face my kindergarten band—a sea of hopeful faces staring at me.

Now this was the point at which it all started to go wrong. I had no idea what I was supposed to do with that flipping baton. I had seen Ricky and Mitch on TV, but with severe four-year-old performance anxiety, I couldn't recall if they twirled it, tossed it, or drew circles with it. I just stood there, baton arm frozen at my side, and started to cry.

Miss Koyle grabbed the baton and started waving it wildly, while the twig-tapping girls began banging their wooden instruments of musical torture. The tune ended, and I slipped away to my seat on the floor, head down, silent.

The next day the teacher called me up to the platform and handed me the baton once again. Oh good, a fresh start! But I still didn't know what to do with that darn baton. So, I cried—again.

Then came the final insult. The teacher called on Raymond, who hadn't even learned how to tie his shoes yet, to take over my job. I had no warning, no probation. She just passed him *my* baton and asked me to sit down with the rest of the faceless, nameless stick bangers. Then Raymond started waving the baton just like I'd seen the conductors do on TV.

Please, Miss Koyle, I've got it now!

I desperately tried to catch the teacher's eye to show her the light had finally come on. But she only had eyes for Raymond, leaving me in the corner with my sticks. I was yesterday's news.

For more than fifty years, I've been swinging that baton in my dreams to see if I can get it right. I can't read a musical note or carry a tune, and my pitch has been off since the birth of my first child. Music was never going to be my career, so my baton failure was probably inconsequential in the scheme of things.

But here's the important stuff that I learned in Miss Koyle's class:

- I learned that firing is just the umpire telling you that you lost the game when all along you were playing poorly and probably knew how it would end anyway.

- I learned that with a bit of help, people could learn to do their jobs much better.
- I learned that career success is possible when your career goals fit your strengths. In other words, don't try to swim upriver—that's for fish.
- I learned that pain dulls with time, and humour carries the day.
- I learned that failures are where life's lessons are learned, so celebrate failure as a character builder.

See—I've got it, Miss Koyle.

BUSTED

It was a beautiful evening as my husband and I walked along the sidewalk enjoying the sights of Cape Town, South Africa.

We were eager to get back to the hotel for a drink and a buffet meal, the first of twenty-eight buffet meals we would have on our tour. I shouldn't be allowed anywhere near buffets because I buffet graze, wanting to sample everything that comes out of the kitchen.

As we walked, we came upon a section where the sidewalk was under construction and the concrete was broken up, so I carefully stepped through the mess, keeping my eyes focused on the ground. My bifocal lenses distort my depth perception when I look down, so I try to be very observant about where I place my feet.

Step. Step. Step. *Oops, watch it, Di!* Step, step … BOOM!

Down I went with the grace of an African elephant. The sole of my right shoe had caught the edge of a slightly raised metal grate on the sidewalk. My arms shot out to try to break my fall, but they buckled under my weight. My knees then smashed into the pavement, as did my abundant bust.

I expected my face to smash into the metal grate next, but it didn't. Miraculously, my boobs had broken my fall—I was busted! They were my own built-in personal protective equipment, performing beyond the call of mammary duty, mainly because my bust was bolstered by substantial cushions of fat. Nature knew what she was doing when she built those things.

I got up quickly, ignoring the scrapes to my hands and sore kneecaps. The only thing worse than tumbling full force into the pavement is having onlookers come to your rescue, making you feel even more embarrassed. At least I wouldn't have to explain any facial scrapes to people who gawked at me.

"No, no, no – it's ok! I'm fine! Not a problem," I chirped to onlookers as I righted myself, trying to pretend that I had never fallen. By the time Honey glanced back to see why I wasn't beside him, I was cautiously walking again—a little bent but not broken. I limped up to him, admitting I had tripped and fallen. Pride goeth when you falleth.

"You're just like your Mother," Honey said, reminding me that Mom had tripped and broken a bone on vacation years ago, likely due to her wearing bifocals as well.

I limped into the hotel, looking forward to a glass of wine that would wash away the pain of my sore limbs. My new tunic top had a huge black stain covering my face-saving mammary cushions, so I quickly buttoned-up my cardigan to hide the evidence of my clumsiness.

We headed into the dining room for yet another buffet dinner which I was determined to enjoy, bruised or not. I tried to be dignified and not eat as though it were "The Last Supper."

For fifteen more days we were on the trip of a lifetime in Africa, so there was no way I was I going to be held back from any activity because of my scrape and bruises. With butt boosts from my Honey, I could even climb up into the safari vehicles with barely a grimace. Fortunately, little walking was needed on our tour, and when we did have to walk, Honey held my hand tightly to keep me upright.

We saw every animal in Africa that we wanted to see from the safety of our safari vehicle except for the leopard, which had not even been seen by our guide in twenty years. But we did see a woman on safari in a knitted leopard-patterned sweater. Close enough.

Our fabulous trip to Africa was not a bust at all.

ALL THUMBS

When my sister Wendy and I lived in Toronto, we went on vacation to Club Med in Cancun where she met her Mr. Right from Vermont. Bob and Wendy soon became engaged then set a wedding date for January 1987. As my other brother-in-law commented at the reception, "Diane got the tan, Wendy got the man."

When you're from a family of four girls, the last thing you need to worry about when you're planning your wedding is finding a maid of honour or bridesmaid. There's always a sister a phone call away who is eager to be one of your wedding attendants if called upon.

I was thrilled when Wendy asked me to be her maid of honour. It couldn't be that difficult, right? I wanted to coordinate my dress with the bouquets of large French tulips she planned, so I had a seamstress make a bright pink frock which blossomed out from the waist like an upside-down tulip. I was going to be pretty in pink.

The wedding day arrived. Seventy-five friends and relatives stood smiling as they watched Wendy and me descend the large circular stairway from the second-floor dressing area to join the minister, the groom, the best man, and the wedding guests.

We didn't trip, we didn't fall. So far, so good.

The ceremony began with the minister speaking her introductory words. She then turned and asked me for the groom's ring which I had put on my thumb for safe keeping. I looked at my thumb for the ring, but there was no ring. I looked at my other thumb, but again, no ring.

Panic stricken, I looked at Wendy and whispered that I couldn't find the ring. She stared at me in amazement, her eyes bugging out. I faced the guests who were waiting expectantly for me to give the ring to the minister. This circus was not Wendy's vision of how their beautiful wedding would go.

I blurted out to everyone in the room, "About the ring—I can't find it! The ring must have flown off my thumb when I was talking with my hands!"

All the guests and the wedding party turned their eyes to the floor, searching desperately around their feet for the airborne band of gold. Suddenly, from across the room, the groom's father yelled, "I found it!" to great laughter from the wedding guests. He picked up the flying sphere and handed it to the minister.

The wedding ceremony then picked up where it had left off, and soon both Wendy and Bob were wearing their new wedding rings, with no thanks to me.

Not surprisingly, that was the last time I was invited to be in anyone's wedding party, although our youngest son recently chose me to walk his yellow Labrador retriever, Murphy, complete with his bow tie, down the aisle when he married his bride, Taylor. The dog and I made a fine-looking couple if I do say so myself.

But maybe the ring misadventure was a good luck omen. Wendy, married 34 years to Bob, is the only one of the four sisters who has not been divorced, so my other two divorced sisters might want to consider including me in their wedding parties for good luck if they ever decide to marry again.

Neither of them have dogs, so they won't need me as their canine escort, but I am an experienced, though slightly incompetent, maid of honour.

PASSING THE TORCH

It was a beautiful summer day, so my Love God and I decided to take a drive through the North Carolina countryside. Surprisingly, we found ourselves talking about funerals, cremations, online bill paying, and finances, things that people often talk about as they get older so that they know their partner's thoughts and wishes.

My Love God has expressed a wish to be cremated, stored in a fishing tackle box, then sprinkled on the salmon fishing grounds off the coast of British Columbia in Canada. This is a long way from North Carolina, so the tackle box urn and I would have to board a plane and hightail it to BC after the service. I would keep the tackle box urn stored safely in my tote bag under the airplane seat—I mean, what if I put him in the overhead bin and a careless passenger accidentally knocked his ashes out of the urn before we reached his final resting place with the salmon? One thing I know for sure is that my Love God does not wish to be sprinkled in row 22, seat D, on American Airlines Flight 1729.

As we were discussing these delicate topics, it hit me that I shouldn't get all of him cremated. Instead, I would like to keep his most valuable appendage close by to use whenever I needed it. Honey agreed that this would be a good idea, and that I would need to ask the cremator person to carefully chop off the appendage after Honey passed. I think Honey was even touched by my desire to keep a part of him with me forever. We still haven't figured out how to keep the appendage stiff so that it works effectively after he passes, so this may be a problem. It's a wonderful thing when a husband and wife can talk about such matters, isn't it?

At this point, I feel that I should explain how we came to this unusual decision. You see, when our talk involves Honey's passing on, it also involves talk of how bills will continue to get paid online, because Honey works that way. Much of that stuff eludes me and—I'm being brutally honest here—I'm a fossil, as our youngest son calls me. I still even use a little black leather address book—just cross off the old address and phone number whenever the friend moves and add the new information—I've done this for years. My little black book is like a little history book. Can't do that in a fancy little iPhone, now can you?

So, despite my desire to avoid technology talk in this life and the next, Honey told me for the umpteenth time that there were some things that I needed to be able to do in case he passed through the pearly gates unexpectedly—things like using his passwords, account numbers, websites, and all the stuff that the CFO of our house uses to keep track of our spending and piggy bank balance. Now this was when I went into shock—Honey revealed that he uses his fingerprint to access certain financial accounts. *Oh great!* This may work well for him right now, but if he passes and is cremated, I am snookered.

This revelation then prompted us to discuss the best way to pass the financial torch to me, and that's when we decided it would be best if we just chopped off his finger after he passes, and then when it stiffened a little, I could use his fingerprint to access our accounts, just like he does. No switching fingerprints, passwords, and all that complicated stuff. Chop, chop—and then I could continue performing the CFO duties in our house without missing a beat.

You *did* think I meant his finger, didn't you?

CHECK TWICE,
PHONE ONCE

I looked like a sheepdog with my shaggy grey hair hanging over my face. *It's time for a haircut,* I declared to myself. I would first check if my favourite stylist was working that day.

Doing a Google search, I found the phone number for the "Great Clips" hair salon in "Waterford," a neighbourhood in the town of Leland where I live.

I clicked on the phone number and a cheery young woman answered, "Great Clips, Waterford."

"Good morning," I responded in my equally cheery voice. "Is Caitlin working today?" Caitlin has cut my fine, grey hairlets in a blunt cut for four years. She understands my hairlets and they do as she tells them.

"There isn't a Caitlin working here," the young woman responded.

"Oh, so she isn't working today?" I clarified.

"No, there isn't a Caitlin working here at all. We have a Kathy, a Courtney, a Suzy, a Jill and an Emily."

I thought I noticed a slight touch of impatience in her voice, or maybe it was in my voice. Maybe she had a customer in her chair who was glaring at her to get her off the phone.

"Well, my husband was there a week ago and Caitlin cut his hair. Perhaps she quit in the last week." I realized I was getting a tad snarky, but I didn't care. This woman was getting on my last nerve. *I ought to know who has been cutting my hair and my Honey's hair for the past four years, Missy.*

The young woman responded politely but firmly. "I have worked here for many years, Ma'am, and we have never had a Caitlin working here."

I felt like I was in an episode of the *Twilight Zone* or maybe *Candid Camera*. How could I help this confused woman understand that Caitlin works there? I decided to try a new approach. "Is this the Great Clips in Waterford near the Harris Teeter grocery store in Leland?"

There was a long pause. "No, we're actually near the Subway sandwich place in Waterford."

She just pushed my food button. I know where every sandwich place is in Leland NC because submarine sandwiches happen to be one of my favourite food delicacies. I know there is a Subway restaurant at a nearby gas station in Leland but there is no hair salon of any kind there—just a convenience store with snacks like beef jerky and spicy sweet chili Doritos.

The young woman on the phone tried again. "Ma'am I don't know where this Leland place is that you're talking about, but we're the Great Clips in Waterford, Wisconsin."

Wisconsin? How did I end up calling Wisconsin?

I couldn't get off the phone fast enough. "Oh geez. I'm so sorry to have bothered you— I made a mistake. Happy New Year. Bye."

I grabbed my phone and googled Great Clips, Waterford. There were five such listings in the U.S.: Waterford, CT; Waterford, WI; Waterford, Grand Rapids MI; Waterford, Dublin CA and of course Waterford, Leland NC. Who knew there were so many Waterfords?

It seems that when I googled Great Clips, Waterford, I clicked on the phone number that was shown underlined and in blue letters, which took me straight to Great Clips …in Wisconsin! If I had looked at the phone number carefully, I might have noticed that it had an area code in a state halfway across the country.

I learned an important lesson from my careless mistake, which wasted both my time as well as the Wisconsin hairdresser's time. My hairdresser, Caitlin, is a great hairdresser because she *measures twice, cuts once.* In the future I will *check twice, phone once.*

No more phone calls to hairdressers in Wisconsin.

LAUGHING MATTERS

Her comment came out of left field.

"I think I'll jump off the bridge near the village," my 90-year-old mother said as I was about to eat a spoonful of Raisin Bran, the kind with granola clusters.

"Mom, what are you talking about?"

"When I'm ready to go, I think I'll just walk up the street with my walker, turn left at the stoplight then jump off the bridge."

Good heavens! Mom had been feeling her age ever since she had broken her hip a few months earlier. She had good days and bad days as is common with people her age. It was time to lighten up this conversation.

"But Mom, you'll land with a big splash in the Thames River, and you know how much you hate swimming. Just think what it would do to your hair! And if it's winter, you could end up on a snow-covered ice floe floating all the way to Lake St. Clair which would be a very cold trip—and you know how you hate the cold. So, what were you planning to wear on your jump?"

"I think I'll wear my fluffy pajamas and my red puffy coat with the fur around the hood—it's really warm," she declared.

"Yes, that sounds perfect Mom, but it's at least a mile to the bridge from here. That's a long way to walk with your walker." She hadn't even walked around her cul-de-sac in years, so she was being a bit optimistic about walking to the bridge.

"Is it really that far?" she wondered aloud. "I've never walked that far with my walker. Maybe I'll need to phone for a taxi."

I'd love to be eavesdropping on that call to the dispatcher when Mom asks for a taxi to take her to the middle of the bridge.

"I have a better idea. You can go out to the back yard and roll down the hill into the river. Then you don't have to walk to the bridge."

"That sounds much better!" she said with a smile.

"When were you planning to do this, Mom?"

"Oh, one day when I feel like the end is here. Or maybe when I get tired of eating macaroni and cheese for dinner." She loves mac and cheese so if she gets sick of it, it could be that the end is extremely near.

"Well, Mom, Grandma lived to be 100 years old, and her brother lived to 105—you're only 90, so you'll probably live a long time if heredity has anything to do with it.

"I'm 90? I thought I was 78," she said. Bless her heart.

"Mom, I'm quite sure you'll die one day either sitting on the sofa watching TV or in bed because those are the only places you ever go. Just be sure to apply your lipstick every morning so that you look your best in case you pass that day."

"You're right," she said. "I'd be much more comfortable just lying on the sofa or in bed when the end is near, maybe watching a Cary Grant movie on TV. Yes, that's how I'd like to go, and I'll be sure to put my lipstick on every morning. I'll live each day like it might be my last. One more thing, Diane—at my funeral, I want to wear my padded bra so that my boobs look big."

"Shall do, Mom." I think she was embracing her new departure plan.

Looking over at the clock, I noticed that it was 5:00 PM, and figured that my little grey-haired mama was probably getting hungry.

"Do you want macaroni and cheese for dinner, Mom? If you don't want it, just say so, but whatever you do please don't roll down the hill into the river to end your life just because I offered you some mac and cheese for dinner. I can make you a hot dog - you like hot dogs.

By then we were both laughing, which was a good thing, because it's hard to both laugh and feel like you want to die.

SECOND VERSE, SAME AS THE FIRST

Since the pandemic began, I have had nowhere to go and nothing much to do. In my desire to avoid doing real housework, I decided to go through the contents of five old shoeboxes hidden behind my clothes in the closet.

Buried in the boxes were birthday cards, mementos, little notebooks, and photos, but I also found several elementary school report cards which I hadn't seen in more than fifty years. *These should make fascinating reading,* I mused. I arranged them by grade so I could see how much I had progressed over the years—or not.

I started by reading my kindergarten report card. I was almost a straight A kindergarten student, except for one subject. Miss Koyle gave me a B for "Sings in tune." Today I'd likely get a C. Oops, Honey just corrected me— I'd get a D.

Miss Koyle also wrote that I wasn't as enthusiastic in second term as I was in the first term. Had she forgotten that she fired me as the rhythm band conductor, then put me in the back row of the band banging the rhythm sticks? *I think that alone would account for my lack of enthusiasm, Miss Koyle!*

But she also commented that my handwork was neat, which was the first and last time a teacher would say that about my handwork.

Despite my inability to carry a tune or conduct the rhythm band, I managed to get promoted into the first grade with Miss Whitcroft. I can recall telling my parents, after my first day in grade one, that I was in the "high grade one." How would a five-year-old know that she had been placed in the class with the higher-level students, my folks wondered?

I didn't know that at all, I told Mom. The other first grade class was on the first floor, while my grade one class was on the second floor, so that meant I was in the "high" grade one class...*that's what high means, right Mom?*

Miss Whitcroft wrote on my Grade 1 report card in first term that I was progressing well: I was slow and easy going, but always kept at my work until it was done. By year-end, she was concerned that my printing was extremely poor, and had become worse as the year went on. This would be the first verse of an awfully familiar song.

Missing from the shoe boxes were my second and third grade report cards which was unfortunate as they may have been my best report cards. *We'll never know, will we?*

On my fourth-grade report card, my teacher, Mrs. Bycroft, wrote that I was "very ambitious, a good worker, pleasant, but easily disappointed." I knew what she meant: I cried a lot. Teachers made me nervous if they got too close to me, so I often ended up crying for no obvious reason. I can't explain it even now, more than sixty years later. Then came that familiar report card refrain: "Diane's printed work could be more carefully done." *Second verse, same as the first.*

But on my end-of-year report card, Mrs. Bycroft played a new tune: I was an excellent student and my writing had improved—she still couldn't say it was good. Maybe I was starting to get the hang of handwriting!

Apparently, I wasn't getting the hang of it at all according to my Grade 5 report cards.

In fifth grade, I also took grade six subjects as I was in the "accelerated" program. My teacher, Mrs. Kelly, who overwhelmed the class with projects, book reports and tests, said on my first report card that my writing was poor and carelessly done *Third verse, same as the first.*

But on my final report card, she had some positive comments—math, phonics, and reading were good, and my English composition grades were terrific, perhaps foretelling that creative writing could be in my future. But she ended my report on a negative note—I was an enthusiastic worker, but at times had a carefree attitude about my work. *That's how I survived the year from hell with you, Mrs. Kelly,* I recalled with pain.

Seventh grade was a new beginning. I had my first male teacher, Mr. Ayearst, who didn't worry about the aesthetics of my writing, but was more interested in the substance of what I wrote. It was refreshing not to read negative comments about my handwriting—my report cards started to sound positive.

Now, more than fifty years later, my handwriting is worse than ever, but keyboards have leveled the playing field. I now handwrite for speed and for free flow thinking, but I type for ease of reading and editing. The only time I really need to use cursive writing these days is to sign birthday cards or bank checks, and nobody who receives those items cares about my handwriting.

The world finally figured out what I knew all along as a child: beautiful handwriting is not that important in the long run of life, but what you say, do and write is.

Are you listening, Miss Whitcroft?

THIS WASN'T
HAYLEY'S CAMP

In July 1961, sister Janet and I went to a summer camp for the first time along with two neighbourhood friends, Margaret, and Nancy. They had heard about Huron Church Camp from their local church, then told my sister and me all about it. We told our parents, begging to go too. At only $11 a week per child, our parents figured this would be the least expensive camp experience they could find for us. They were all in.

The first day of camp finally arrived. We put our carefully packed bags in the trunk of Dad's car, ready for the one-hour drive. We didn't know much about summer camp except what we had seen in "The Parent Trap" when Hayley Mills went to camp, where she found out that she had a twin sister. Our camp didn't look at all like Hayley's camp. The water in our drinking fountains tasted like sulfur and our meals were very plain. Hayley would have hightailed it out of there for sure.

We settled into our cabin with six other girls and our two counsellors. I had packed a Nancy Drew mystery book and even a dictionary so I could add to my list of homonyms that I had started in grade four— I was not cool. Our days were filled with swimming in the lake, doing arts and crafts, sitting around campfires, and playing baseball. We also went to church out in the woods three times a day, sitting on benches and running our toes through the sandy soil.

Janet, Margaret, Nancy, and I signed up as a group to be in a talent show one night, singing a Kumbaya-type song we all knew. We swayed back and forth, undoubtedly out of rhythm with each other. Under stress, Margaret, a shy but very smart girl, peed on stage during our performance. We finished our song, then quietly left the stage to polite applause.

When camp was over, Dad picked us up then we drove back home. That was when Janet and I found out that we had been snookered. Our parents and two younger sisters had gone on a road trip where they stayed in a motel with a pool and ate in restaurants every day, something we had never done. It sounded like so much fun and we were envious.

Fast forward sixty years to a recent social media conversation in which our two younger sisters declared that their road trip was even better than we had been told. They didn't stay in a motel, they boasted, but in a resort like the one in "Dirty Dancing!" Heck, we could have danced with the likes of Patrick Swayze if we had been there, sister Janet and I thought. Our younger sisters then added insult to injury by telling us about their cute teenage activity director who took them boating, and on hayrides, along with other fun activities. I am certain they didn't go to church three times a day or drink sulfur water from a water fountain like we did.

Janet and I are unable to confirm our sisters' recollections of their supposed resort vacation because Dad has passed, and Mom has memory issues, but we think that our evil younger sisters' memories have been enhanced for the purpose of making Janet and me jealous. It worked, even after all these years.

But Janet and I have memories of that church camp that our younger sisters will never have, which makes us special too. We have been to resorts and restaurants as adults, but our summer camp experience was a once in a lifetime event for two young girls.

BOO-BOO WAKES UP

Just went I thought I knew it all I found out I didn't. A trip to England with Honey opened my eyes to the world of tortoises. Not the little ones I had seen in North America but a ten-inch pet —hardly cuddly, but incredibly interesting.

I had never been to England until one March about thirty years ago. We were eager to visit my husband's relatives in Manchester, which was his birthplace. His aunt Muriel and his cousin Ian had a narrow little house in which the curtains, paintings, sofas, and wallpaper were all blooming with flowers which were not in the same floral print or even the same colours. Classic British décor—very cozy, but a bit dizzying to look at.

Muriel not only had two grown sons, but as we found out during our visit, she had a pet tortoise, which she pronounced "tortoys"—maybe that's a British thing, but more likely it's a Muriel thing.

We learned that the tortoise, named Boo-Boo, was forty years old, though he didn't look a day over thirty to me. Muriel explained that pet tortoises like Boo-Boo can live to be 100 years of age, which means that owners need to have a succession plan for the care of their tortoises who would likely outlive at least two of their owners.

Then came the biggest shock of all. In England, pet tortoises, originally from warmer countries, hibernate all winter. They apparently bulk up on food before their winter hibernation, although I'm not sure I'd know a bulked-up tortoise if I saw one.

Boo-Boo was still hibernating when we visited in March, but much to our amazement, Muriel announced that it was time for Boo-Boo's spring release, so she would awaken him while were there!

She took us to a shed at the back of her house, and there on a shelf, was a round cake tin, the ubiquitous kind that fruitcakes come in at Christmas. The tin was wrapped in a blanket to help insulate Boo-Boo against the chilly English nights, and he had been placed on a bed of newspapers. Little holes were punched in the lid to ensure there was ventilation for Boo-Boo while he slept. The lid was securely closed with heavy-duty wrapping tape, perhaps to prevent the tortoise's escape in case he decided he had slept long enough and wanted to get up for some breakfast.

Muriel brought the hibernating Boo-Boo into the kitchen in his cake tin, then removed the wrapping tape. She carefully lifted the tortoise out of his tin into shallow warm water in the sink. His legs started to move as soon as he was set in the warm water. His eyes were stuck shut so she thoroughly washed his eyes with Dettol to clean away the yuck. Boo-Boo was ready to go!

We followed Muriel outside to the back yard where she set Boo-Boo free to walk on the spring grass. He waddled along the garden's edge, appearing to tilt oddly to one side. Upon closer examination, Muriel found that Boo-Boo's right rear foot had been folded awkwardly underneath him during his long hibernation in the tin. It would take a few days for him to walk the kink out, she said.

When Muriel passed away many years later, Boo-Boo was cared for by her son Ian. The tortoise would be about seventy by now, so Ian, also about seventy, recently gave Boo-Boo to a young girl he knew in the neighbourhood because he was moving to an apartment. He wanted to rehome Boo-Boo with a younger caregiver in the event the tortoise lived to be one hundred years of age. Ian explained to the little girl about Boo-Boo's hibernation, the importance of tucking his feet in the tin carefully and his wake-up routine every spring. Life for Boo-Boo would continue as it had for his first seventy years.

I have some advice for people who are thinking of getting a pet tortoise: if you aren't prepared to have a pet who hibernates all winter and may live to be one hundred years of age, get yourself a goldfish or a hamster.

LIFE ISN'T ALWAYS PEACHES AND CORN

Early one afternoon my Love God decided that he would like some corn on the cob and fresh peaches to go with the baked chicken that we were going to have for dinner. Sometimes we have the food on hand for dinner, but this time we didn't.

Off we drove to the grocery store, buying not only these foods but another $100 worth of food including pretzels and cheese puffs. That's what happens when we don't stick to our grocery list.

An hour later at home Honey asked me where the peaches were.

"Probably on the counter," I replied, not remembering putting them anywhere.

He shook his head. "Nope, not there."

I hated pointing out the obvious to this highly intelligent man but did anyway. "Did you happen to look in the fruit and vegetable drawers in the fridge?"

I heard the fridge drawers open while he checked them. "Nope, not there either," he declared.

Knowing where things are kept in the kitchen is not Honey's strength. Just yesterday he asked me where the dishcloths were kept, which tells you a lot, given we have lived in this house for three years and the dishcloths have been in the same drawer the entire time.

"Well, maybe they're in the fridge in the garage." Little did I think I needed to have memorized every place I put the groceries.

The door to the garage shut with a thud. "Nope, not there," he said, sounding like a broken record.

Good heavens! *There are only so many places that the peaches and the corn can be, Honey.*

Perhaps they hadn't even made it out of the car. "Why don't you check the car trunk and back seat." *Do I have to do all the thinking around here?* I asked myself.

"Nope, not there either," he said after returning from the garage.

Jeepers. If I need to get off the sofa to recheck everywhere that he said he looked, there will be trouble in the love nest.

As I sat there munching on my pretzels, I began to wonder if there was one last place the peaches and corn could be but shouldn't be. I got up slowly, then nonchalantly walked over to the kitchen fridge, opening the bottom freezer door quietly so Honey wouldn't hear me.

There, on top of the hunks of frozen ground turkey and ice-covered mixed vegetables, were three ears of fresh corn and three peaches—right where I had put them when my brain left my body.

I'm so sorry for thinking that you weren't looking carefully, Honey! One day I would explain to him where I had put the corn and peaches, but as he had moved on from the search for peaches and corn to watching his favourite fishing show, I didn't feel the need to confess my blunder right then.

But I still think he should have known where the dishcloths have been kept for the last three years.

THE NAME GAME

Since publishing two books of personal humour essays, I've had many opportunities to meet people at craft fairs, book clubs and other speaking events. Local magazines have kindly put my photo on their covers, requiring me to fluff up my hair and hold my head in that special way that minimizes the number of chins people can see.

But it still surprises me that people often recognize me out in the community when I'm not waving my books around or wearing my wiener dog tee shirt.

One day when I was walking out of a store towards my car, a woman I didn't know quietly said, "I love your lipstick book," as she walked by me. More recently a woman in the pots and pans aisle of the local department store said, "You're the lipstick lady, right? I have both your books."

A lady at the town hall paying her property tax bill recognized me too. I am not used to this attention.

But it doesn't stop there. I was walking the dog at the beach when a woman stopped to tell me that I was on the cover of a magazine on her coffee table at home. The next day, a young man at a computer repair shop told me the same thing. I even saw my face on a magazine lying on an end table at a used furniture store. I get around it seems.

But this local recognition has caused me some uncomfortable moments too. One summer evening, I was having dinner at a downtown restaurant with two friends when a woman and her partner entered the restaurant where they sat at a nearby table. I glanced over at these diners but didn't recognize them.

Suddenly the woman stood up, smiled, and waved at me. *Oh, no. I thought. Here comes trouble. I don't know this woman, but she is behaving like she knows me. Think, Diane, think!*

"Hi there Diane. I haven't seen you in such a long time!"

Oh no! What do I say to this woman? My Pinocchio nose started to grow. There might have even been a little sweat ball hanging off the end of it.

"Yes, it really has been a while! Nice to see you!" I replied with a big smile.

"What have you been up to lately?" she asked. I was on safe ground here as my answer would be the same whether I knew her or not.

"Well, I've been at some craft fairs with my husband, and we were up in Canada visiting my Mom. How about you—what have you been doing?" Her answer might give me a clue about who she was.

Nah-uh. No clue. "Well, we've been traveling a bit and getting ready for our kids' visit."

It was now my turn to talk in this ping-pong conversation, but I was stuck for words. I needed to end this before I exposed my failed memory.

"Well, I should get back to my dinner, but it's been so great seeing you again!" I gave her a big smile as well as a lady hug with a pat on the back as though I were burping a baby.

I returned to my dinner and my two friends, whose names I really did know.

HOW PRISONS ROLL

I've been thinking a lot about prison lately. Not because I have engaged in any criminal activity but because of a recent news article that said a new prisoner like Felicity Huffman would be allowed one roll of toilet paper every two weeks. That didn't sound like much to me, so I decided to analyze this a bit further. I'm nimble with addition and subtraction but my business degree kicks in when multiplication or division skills are required.

The first question I have is: what size of toilet paper roll are they talking about exactly— a roll with 1000 sheets or a roll with 231 sheets like the ones in our guest bathroom? My next question is: how many times would an inmate visit the throne each day? Let me think about my own habits…one, two, three… ok, we'll say that I visit seven times a day.

So, here's the math: A roll of TP with 1000 sheets would mean a prisoner could use an average of seventy-one sheets per day, or about ten sheets per visit. But if it were a roll with only 231 sheets, then a prisoner could only use about sixteen sheets per day on average, or just over two sheets per visit.

That small roll would be a major problem for most people, and particularly for women. It might work well enough for men who use the shaking method for their number one visits but shaking won't work for women.

Maybe prisoners can do prison work like laundry or gardening to earn more rolls in case they are big dumpers or have other problems. Or maybe their relatives can chip in to put money in the inmate's tuck shop account to allow them to buy extra toilet paper. Of course, the prisoner might have to give up a Mars bar or Diet Coke each week if their tuck money runs low, but they need to understand they can't have everything, and are in no position to negotiate.

But maybe the prison gives extra toilet paper as a reward for good prisoner behaviour— a win-win for everyone I'd say.

I'm still not sure why toilet paper has to be rationed in prison. Do prisons fear that a prisoner could use a roll of toilet paper to pummel the prison guard, then steal his keys to the cells? Or is it about the cost? If it is, prisons could economize be using one ply rather than two ply toilet paper.

Reading about this toilet paper rationing has motivated me to never end up in prison. I wonder if Felicity Huffman or Lori Laughlin thought about this before they paid to get their daughters into college?

Everybody needs to consider this before they decide to rob a bank, commit murder, or kidnap someone, especially if they have a delicate system. Schools should give presentations to high school kids before they get in trouble to warn them that the prison toilet paper doesn't go far. They don't want to have to explain that to their tushes.

HONEY KNOWS BEST

The sharp pain in my shoulder came on amazingly quickly that night right after dinner. It hurt when I took a deep breath, so I switched to shallow breaths. I changed positions. I walked around the yard, taking little breaths. I tried to minimize the problem because if Honey gets wind that something isn't right with me, he's like a dog on a bone.

Nurse Honey suddenly kicked in. "What's wrong?" he asked me. I told him about the persistent shoulder pain. I knew what was coming. "I think we should go to the hospital, Di."

Oh jeepers! Not this again. Why did I say anything?

That man has a long memory. Two years ago, I had a pain in my side and after much debating, I finally agreed to go to the ER because it was so much easier than arguing with him. After a few hours in the ER, the doctor told me I had kidney cancer. As a result of this experience, I have vowed not to argue with my Love God anymore when he suggests that we go to the hospital. Honey knows best.

As expected, we then drove to the hospital. Out of nowhere he asked, "Do you think this pain has anything to do with the dinner I cooked tonight?"

Oh my gosh! I only wished this pain were as simple as indigestion which his excellent dinner had not created in any way.

We arrived at the ER where they asked me a few questions mostly related to the corona virus which is a much bigger concern for hospitals these days than a shoulder pain.

"Have you been out of the country recently?" the nurse asked me.

"Yes, we went to Africa," I stated, naming the four countries we visited, even feeling a bit worldly as the nurse expressed awe. After many questions, they were satisfied that I didn't have the virus.

Then they whisked me off to a private room, where they put what looked like twelve little sticky notes on my arms, legs, chest, neck, and tummy. Then they hooked me up to some beeping machines, did a scan and an EKG.

The cardiologist asked me if I had any health conditions. None really, I thought, except maybe for being fattish, which he could certainly see for himself under all my sticky notes. I thought carefully for a few seconds and finally said almost as an afterthought, "Well, I do have kidney cancer."

"Oh really? Well, that would certainly be a useful thing to mention! Tell me about it." I gave him the one breath version of that adventure. The cancer is not top of mind with me because I feel fine. Every six months the doctor analyzes some x-rays and blood work to see if it has spread, which it hasn't. So far so good.

I suddenly became aware that the shoulder and side pain had disappeared, which I told the nurse when she appeared. I texted Honey with my pain update.

He said that if I sprinted to the front door, still wearing the twelve sticky notes, he would drive up, snatch me, then we'd make a run for it. Coming soon on Netflix: "Honey and Di Escape from the Hospital."

The cardiologist, who had examined all my test results with the radiologist, returned to tell me that everything looked fine. Maybe "Pleuritic Chest." Maybe a pinched nerve.

"Let's get you out of here before you get the virus." No argument from me. I summoned my husband by text, and he drove up to the ER door.

"They said they didn't think it was your cooking but that it might be a smart idea for you to cook our dinners for a week just to be sure," I said with a smile.

He smiled back. His name is Honey, not Sucker.

CONVERSATIONS BETWEEN PLANETS

People often say "men are from Mars and women are from Venus" when describing differences in the behaviours of men and women.

These differences seem to be most noticeable in couples' approaches to technology. If Honey had not dragged me into this century, I would still be using a rotary dial princess phone in bubblegum pink.

In a typical technology conversation in our house, I will say to Honey, "I can't make my laptop do what it has always done, and I don't know why. I have clicked everywhere and checked the whatchamacallit three times, but I still can't make it work. I'm sure that I have done something wrong."

I add this last sentence to avoid his saying, "It doesn't change on its own, Diane." I take the blame, declare myself a dunce, and wait for him to save the day, technologically speaking.

Complete with deep sighs, his response usually starts with, "Does it have to be done right now? I'm watching (*pick one*) hockey/football/ this movie/ the news," or "I'm trying to type this email—could it wait?" to which I humbly respond, "Of course, Honey. Just let me know when it's a good time. I'll keep working on it and maybe I'll figure it out."

I can be very patient when I'm desperate.

Finally, Honey takes over the operation of the offending device and clicks on places I didn't know existed while I watch, trying to learn his techno-secrets. He hands the device back to me then announces in a fake officious voice, "Technical Support is on a lunch break. Please leave a message or take a ticket number for support."

I ignore my techno-love-god and continue my interrogation, "But what did you do to fix the thingamajig?"

"I rebooted it." That's the answer to almost all technical problems in our house.

My ineptness goes well beyond my laptop and phone, of course. The other day I heard Honey telling the phone company service person that we absolutely need cable TV in our house and, yes, he knew he could stream the shows.

Then he said to the service person, "Someone in this house needs to be able to press a button on a remote to get a cable channel and she is sitting right in front of me, so I don't want to say anymore." This Venusian is happy to be excluded from the conversation.

The technological tools in our house have multiplied like rabbits. A new fancy thingamabob has replaced our simple room thermometer and heating/air conditioning control device. Honey can change the house temperature from our living room or from Africa, and it can even be programmed to reduce the air conditioning during the expensive hours so that we can save $1.33 each month.

We also have a new doorbell which is more than just a doorbell. With a normal doorbell, a visitor presses the button, it rings, the dog barks and I answer the door. But Honey has programmed his phone so he can see via the new doorbell who has come to the door, at what time and what package they may have left. He can also chat to the visitor through the doorbell from anywhere in the world, which he has done on more than one occasion.

Nah. I'll just stick to my doorbell and my door barker.

Even with a simple appliance, like our new coffee maker, interplanetary coaching is needed. He shows me how it works, then I try it. The next day, I try to do it by myself, but I usually can't recall which buttons to press in what order, so I ask for a tune-up lesson.

This has been our techno-routine with any new appliances such as our vacuum, but also with new apps on my phone. He learns the technology first, then I get a lesson—ok, maybe three or four lessons.

But just because they make it and sell it, doesn't mean we must own it, in my opinion. Sometimes there's a simpler way to get a perfectly reasonable result with less angst, at least for Venusians. I'm confident that Honey and I can make our interplanetary technologies work for us if he is alive. But what if he isn't?

If Honey leaves this world before me, I'll need to hire a 10-year-old techno-child to take over Honey's duties fixing our technological thingamajigs.

This young talent will be my new Techno-Honey.

IT'S ALL IN HOW YOU SAY IT

The young kid at the grocery store checkout had just finished ringing up the avocados, pigs in a blanket, and bag of egg noodles—the ones without the egg yolks. Norman, as his Food Tiger badge indicated, seemed uncomfortable as he shifted back and forth from foot to foot. I was wondering if he might have an itch that he was dying to scratch but had thought better of it because his mother had probably said, "Norman, don't touch yourself in public!"

Norman looked across the conveyer belt, staring at me directly in the eye through my bifocals. He said without hesitation, "And your senior citizen's discount today is three dollars and forty-three cents."

Whoa! Wait just one minute, Norman-with-an-itch. Who said anything about my being a senior citizen? I sure don't recall you asking my age or asking if I was over sixty but possibly under one hundred. That itchy cashier kid had said "senior citizen" like it was obvious, as if the whole grocery store knew for certain that I was a senior citizen. You'd think I had it tattooed on my forehead, for heaven's sake. That boy didn't even allow for the possibility that maybe, just maybe, I was a few weeks or even months under the "age of seniority," whatever that was in this store.

Exactly what age are we talking about, Norman? Age sixty-five, when Medicare kicks in? Age sixty-two, when you can start collecting back your forty years of social security contributions? Age sixty, when you sound a whole lot older than you do at fifty-nine? Did you learn to guess ages at the state fair and then hand out stuffed toy giraffes when you got it wrong, Norm? Maybe you owe me a giraffe. Ever think of that, Norm?

I mean, Norman had to be making a wild guess based on…what? My greyish hair mottled with some dark hairlets? My very slightly sagging turkey neck? The hot coral lipstick bleeding into my lip creases? I mean, those things can happen at forty-nine or fifty-three or fifty-seven, can't they? These are not legal evidence of age that Norman should use to certify me as senior. Shouldn't I have to present a special card declaring "I'm a senior" if I am one?

I wanted to scream, "Hey, look at the facts, Norman. I have a paying job, and I have a kid completing four and a half years of college. So how can you, a young whippersnapper, know for sure that I'm a senior citizen? And for the record, the name Norman sounds much older than Diane, so maybe you should get the discount too, based on your old name, Norm."

I don't know what they teach cashiers in cash-register school about good customer relations, but I can assure you that Normie must have snoozed through that lesson. Does he not get that women are extremely sensitive about their age, their looks, and how well their eighty-dollar-per-ounce antiaging cream is working? The question that was on my mind, forcing me to bite my tongue until it bled, was this: How old did Norman think I was?

I faced every woman's difficult dilemma. If I asked Norm how old he thought I was, just to satisfy my vanity and curiosity, he might guess older than I really was. Then I would feel depressed, compelled to get TV's "Lifestyle Lift," and spend all our retirement savings to look non-senior-like, which would then prevent us from going on that RV vacation to Yellowstone that Honey has been dreaming about. But I just can't face the tourists in the RV park looking older than I am, now can I? Norman really opened a can of marital worms.

I'd bet my last buck that Norm would even say to a woman with a tubby tummy, "When is the baby due?" which any man worth his whiskers knows not to ask unless the woman is humming lullabies or is in labour in the breakfast cereal aisle.

So, here's my advice to Norman on the topic of senior citizens: When in doubt, leave it out. To the next young-ish "old lady" who approaches your cash register, say, "It's too bad you don't qualify for the senior citizen's discount, ma'am—you would save three dollars and forty-three cents."

At this point she'd happily proclaim, "But I do qualify, Norman—I really do. I know it's hard to believe, but see my licence?" She'd push the card under his nose. He would then subtract $3.43 from her bill, and she'd walk out of the store with a spring in her step because Norman-with-the-itch thought she was much younger than she really was.

You see, Norman, we'd still get to the bleeping $3.43 discount, but by playing this little game with a woman my age, you'd have a friend and a customer for life.

It's all in how you say it, Norm. Pass it on.

CHANGING THE SUBJECT

My fresh red lipstick was smeared all over my teeth, a look I recognized on my mother who has worn red lipstick all her life. This is one more bit of evidence that I am my mother's daughter.

Mom, age 91, recently moved to a nursing home which we hope will keep her safe, healthy, and happy.

"Is this where I live now?" she asked my older sister, Janet.

"Yes," my sister replied, then changed the subject. Skillful diversion is the best tactic with subjects that are best left alone.

It takes time for a person to adjust to living in a facility with other elderly men and women who all still want some control over their lives. You never know from one day to the next what mood they will be in at their new home.

One day, Mom decided to reserve her favourite two chairs in the common TV room by carving her name into the chairs' armrests with a ballpoint pen so everyone would know they were hers. Then a fellow resident told her he'd, "sit wherever he damn well wanted in the common room," completely ignoring her name on the armrests. Another time, he vowed to kill her. But all residents forget the good and the bad quickly, so altercations fade fast.

A day later, Mom asked why she was in the nursing home and Janet replied she wanted to live there because it was safe and there was lots to do. Good response— Janet then changed the subject.

The following day, Mom called Janet and sister Elaine, screaming that someone had stolen her flowered make up bag, but she had never owned such an item. No point in arguing—just change the subject.

At Christmas, she enjoyed tap dancing in her slippers with bells on the toes, as well as playing bingo and other games. But evenings were difficult, as she would get flustered and confused. The staff identified this as Sundowner Syndrome, which is hard on other residents, family, and staff too.

Mom's memory is getting much worse. One day, she coughed loudly, then looked at my sister and asked, "Who just coughed, you or me?" Oh, geez.

She is calm one moment then agitated the next. She is also smart, funny, and thoughtful. She does her crossword puzzle perfectly every day and can analyze world events with the best of us.

I know in my heart that lipstick on my teeth is not the only thing we have in common. I see myself in my mother in so many ways just as most daughters do and I'll probably be like her when I am her age.

I tell myself: *Be kind, be patient, be funny. Be the daughter that my mother needs me to be at this stage in her life.*

I might even want to give a heads up to my kids on what the future will look like as I age. They will change the subject too, I'm sure.

These are the stages of all our lives—different yet the same.

HIT OR MISS

The urologist's waiting room was filled with ten senior men and me. If I were a single woman, this could be a suitable place to find a date, although any patients here would most likely have plumbing problems given the nature of the medical specialty.

We had all lined up to check in with the receptionist, standing six feet apart as required during this time of social distancing. The men all wore generic light blue masks, while I had a fabric mask covered in red lipstick imprints made for me by my friend, Linda. My lipstick mask was entertaining the staff, who even asked how they might get one. I soon reached the counter where I filled out some forms, then sat down to wait until my name was called.

The atmosphere was lighthearted — a wonderful way for me to avoid worrying about my semi-annual kidney cancer checkup results that the urologist would soon be sharing with me. I have always felt fine before, during and after my kidney cancer surgery.

Just as I was wrapping up my business with the receptionist, she handed me that ubiquitous little transparent plastic bottle with my name written on it so I could supply a urine sample. I quickly drank two dixie cups of water to increase my chances of putting out more than a teaspoon of pee.

I entered the bathroom, locked the door then sat on the commode. I looked around to see if they had pee funnels which many doctors' bathrooms have these days, but there were none, probably because few female patients visit the urologist.

Just for the record, it's difficult for women to aim into that little bottle because it's hard to figure out exactly where the pee comes from. The ten men in the lineup with me will have no problem aiming perfectly with their well-designed equipment.

But women's water works is much more complicated than that of men. For women, it seems to come spraying out from places unknown and splashes all over the bottle, their hands, and the toilet bowl as they try to catch the pee in the little bottle. Today, I'm only able to collect a tablespoon of yellow liquid which I hope will be enough; if not, she'll probably send me back to try again, even though my tank has run dry.

I think that I'll practice at home with a little bottle until I can learn to catch a sample with no splashes or misses. Heck, maybe there's even a YouTube video to show me how to fill the bottle, female style.

Or maybe I'll ask my urologist's assistant to order some pee funnels, women's saving grace for this pee-in-the-bottle exercise. Better yet, perhaps I'll order my own personal plastic pee funnel and keep it in my car's glove compartment for convenience. So much to worry about as I age.

I had some other good news on my visit to the urologist. Not only were my kidney scan results good, but the office staff bought six of my humour books as I was checking out! Forget arts and craft fairs to sell my books- I just need to visit my medical and dental support teams which multiply as I age.

Hmmm... I have two doctors' appointments next week. I think I'll take some of my books with me in case the staff are interested in buying one or two. Beats worrying about pee funnels.

GIVING THANKS, OR NOT

I love Thanksgiving. It's a festive time shared with family, friends, and a turkey.

For Thanksgiving two years ago, we were invited to join with our son's in-laws for dinner on Wednesday, the day before Thanksgiving. We were thrilled to be included in this family event. The food was outstanding—deep fried turkey cooked perfectly accompanied by seven side dishes and desserts. Our son, his wife and her family would then have dinner the following day, the real Thanksgiving Day, with other family members. That's the way Thanksgiving rolls in many households.

With no plans for Thanksgiving Day dinner, we were invited to join our neighbours and another couple for a special Thanksgiving Day buffet dinner at a fine restaurant in Wilmington. You get your money's worth at a buffet, so we signed up. Loosen your belts, comrades!

Originally a reservation had been made for only three couples, but another couple was added at the last minute which required that we move our seating from 2:30 pm to 4:30 pm, the last seating of the day. No problem—we were good to eat anytime.

But just as we were getting in the car to leave for the restaurant, my phone dinged. Our tablemates had arrived a bit early and were informed that the restaurant had run out of turkey. Yes, you read that right—no turkey on Turkey Day. If we wished to go elsewhere for dinner, the restaurant manager said, that would be fine.

Fine? Really? Well, maybe fine for the restaurant but not for us. By 4:30 on Thanksgiving Day any fine restaurant worth its salt and pepper would be fully booked, leaving us with a McDonald's Turkey burger, turkey on a bagel at the Bagel Barn, or if we were lucky, the Turkey Tempura or Coconut Turkey Lo Mein entrees at our local Asian eatery.

The problem was that we were hungry, so staying for the turkey-free Thanksgiving buffet was our only realistic choice. We would fill up with sweet potato casserole, roast beef, and ham, we reasoned, so all was not lost. But as we waited for our table, a staff member sheepishly approached us saying that they had just run out of roast beef.

Huh? Did we hear him correctly or was this a joke to amuse us while we waited? The restaurant should know how many people made a reservation for the buffet, right? Wouldn't they roast extra turkey and roast beef in case some diners ate more than their fair share? Surplus food is never wasted at a restaurant—any chef could turn leftover turkey into Turkey Tetrazzini or unused beef into Beef Stroganoff for weekend diners. What were they thinking?

Oh well, at least this was a fabulous group of friends to _not_ have a turkey dinner with. As we were shown to our table, we stared at each other, feeling helpless and hungry, but I could see in the distance a big hunk of ham on the carving block. *At least there was some kind of meat for our money,* I thought.

After our drink orders were taken, we went to the buffet, eager to load our plates with ham and our choice of sides: mashed potatoes, sweet potatoes, a mysterious casserole, green beans, and roasted Brussel sprouts, although they all looked like they had seen better days. But it was what it was, so we dug into the sadly depleted, room temperature veggies, then lined up for a slice or two of juicy baked ham.

But there was no juicy baked ham, just a honking huge meatless ham bone.

"I'm sorry, ladies and gentlemen. We have just run out of baked ham, but the manager has gone to find some more," said our waiter.

What? Where would the manager find a cooked ham at 5:00 PM on Thanksgiving Day? The only possible answer was that a staff member drove home to grab their own family's ham, leaving their family members eating grilled cheese sandwiches and tomato soup which probably tasted better than the over-heated vegetables anyway.

As we waited for the promised ham, we polished off our veggies. Still hungry, we raided the dessert table. Four desserts later, I was almost full. On principle, however, I was determined to have some ham whenever it arrived.

Arrive it did, at room temperature like everything else. Where had they found this ham? Not in a fridge as it would have been cold; not in their oven as it would have been hot.

The embarrassed wait staff offered us a reduced dinner price of $12.00, down from $32.00 per person which we agreed to— I did have four desserts after all.

The next day each couple in our group wrote a letter to the general manager to say that the holiday dinner was poorly planned and that we were disappointed with our dining experience. She completely agreed and mailed each couple a $100 gift certificate to be used at the restaurant, although it crossed my mind that $100 cash might have been a safer bet for us to use at Bagel Barn. In January, we took a chance and returned to the restaurant where we enjoyed a lovely dinner with the same wonderful friends.

With every calamity that occurs in my life, I learn something. And here's what I learned that year on Turkey Day: People will remember the fun they had with friends long after they can remember what the food was like at dinner.

The joy in life is always about the people you're with.

ROSS THE BOSS

Occasionally, someone you meet makes a big impression on you. This happened one day many years ago when our 3-year-old son met Honey's boss, Ross Norman. Ross had come to our house to borrow our van to move some boxes. Our son answered the door. Ross introduced himself, shaking the young man's hand—probably the little guy's first ever handshake.

A week later, Honey and I were at a big box store where stuffed pandas, brown bears, tigers, and other exotic animals were piled high in a bin. We thought our young son would like the oversized brown bear for his upcoming birthday, as he loved stuff animals. He already had a stuffed German Shepherd dog whom he named, without overthinking it, Shep.

At his birthday party a few days later, we brought in the huge brown bear and his face lit up. He loved this new fuzzy friend which was bigger than he was. But then came the big question—what would he name the bear? He thought long and hard, then announced, "I'm going to call him Ross."

"Did you say Ross?" I asked. This was not a name on most children's radar when naming a stuffed animal.

"Yup—just like Dad's boss."

Really. Ross the stuffed brown bear. Our son hadn't yet learned how to suck up to a boss, even Dad's boss, so I think he must have been intrigued by Ross's name as he had never heard it before – no friends or family members named Ross. And it was certainly an original name for a bear.

But Ross Norman, Honey's boss, gave more than just his name to a bear in our family. When he decided to return to Australia with his new wife, he offered to introduce us to his cleaning woman, Rita, in the event we were interested in having her clean our house.

Good heavens, yes, we said! We then met with Rita so she could assess us and our house. Fortunately, we made her cleaning list.

The day that Rita cleaned our house, Honey arrived home from work, then called me on my cell phone to say he didn't recognize the place. I was slightly hurt, as I didn't think the house looked too bad when I left in the morning because I had cleaned it the night before. That's what we women do—before the cleaning lady arrives, we clean the house, so she doesn't think we're slobs.

Rita came to our house every Wednesday for eleven years, and we went out to dinner every Wednesday for eleven years so we could enjoy our clean kitchen just a wee bit longer.

When we moved to Raleigh, NC in 2004, we asked her to move with us, but her husband said no for some reason. We never had another cleaning lady after Rita.

Ross the Boss was special to our family having been the matchmaker between Rita and us, as well as the namesake for a giant brown bear who was with our family for many years. Maybe somewhere in the world a child has named their pet or stuffed animal "Diane." I can only hope.

SHELTERED FROM THE STORM

The weather report that night said there was a severe storm threat with heavy rain and extraordinarily fierce winds expected early in the evening. We had made plans to go out to dinner with friends, so with our umbrellas and raincoats in the car, we drove off to a local restaurant, leaving our thirteen-year-old dachshund Carley sleeping soundly in her cave-like bed.

She would have to get used to being alone when we'd go to craft fairs or restaurants, because Wyatt, her furry brother from a Labrador Retriever mother, had crossed over the rainbow bridge only one month earlier. Not that they were close, but they seemed to know that their furry sibling had their back.

When we had finished dinner and were leaving the restaurant, lightning flashed and thunder boomed in the sky, sending tremors through the restaurant. I was worried about Carley—she's afraid of thunder and lighting, so I knew she'd be a nervous wreck. I scolded myself, wondering how we could have thought about going out when we knew there was going to be a storm?

We drove home silently in the rain, then pulled up to our darkened house. As we opened the door, multiple cracks of thunder punctuated the rhythm of the rain on the roof.

I glanced over at the diva dachshund's bed near the fireplace, expecting her to leap up, greet us, then dash to the door for a long-awaited pee. But there was no leap, no greet, no dash and no pee. I called her name as I poked my head into her cave, thinking she was cowering in the back. No wiener dog in there.

We searched under the beds, in the closets and the bathrooms, repeatedly calling her name. We yelled the magic word "treat" but even that didn't draw her out. Our house is an open layout with very few places to hide. I've tried hiding—it has never worked.

There was no sign of our black and tan wiener girl in the mud room nor in the adjoining laundry room, but just as we turned around to leave, we heard a faint squeak from the corner of the laundry room. We turned in that direction but didn't see her.

Then came another squeak. We walked towards the noise, and there, hidden under the corner utility sink in a black laundry basket twice her height, buried in a huge pile of cleaning rags, was our wiener dog. Her beady little eyes gleamed in the darkness.

How did our furry girl ever figure out to go to a windowless room and climb into a basket of rags under the sink to feel safe during the thunderstorm? *That wiener girl is smarter than I thought.*

Suddenly she jumped out of her cleaning-rag shelter and dashed to the door to go outside for a pee. Once back inside the house, she doubled back to the kitchen for her Milk-Bone treat. Our girl was back, as confident as ever!

I learned an important lesson that day: next time we go out, we must be sure to leave the laundry room door open so she can access her special storm shelter if necessary. But there is no need to worry about our wiener girl—she's got it!

A TALE OF TWO TOWNS

My sister and her husband have lived in Vermont for 34 years. Exactly where they live in Vermont is hard to say because it keeps changing, and no, they haven't moved.

Wendy is my younger sister who met her husband at Club Med in Cancun when she and I went on vacation. After they married, they lived in a townhouse in a town called White River Junction for 13 years. Then they bought a larger house in Wilder the next town over. One move in 34 years.

When they moved to Wilder, they decided to pay for a Post Office Box at the Post Office. No mailbox at the end of their driveway like most people. For twenty years they drove to the post office to get their mail. I have no idea why they preferred this to having it delivered free to a mailbox in front of their house.

But two weeks ago, Wendy she said they no longer wanted to pay for a Post Office Box, so they installed a mailbox at the end of their driveway beside the road. She asked us to please use her Wilder street address when mailing things to her from now on. No problem, I said, and changed her mailing address in my iPhone contacts list.

Yesterday it all changed—again. Wendy sent a text saying that the mailing address she gave us was wrong. Neither FedEx nor UPS had made deliveries to their new mailbox in the prior two weeks, which was puzzling to her.

The answer to her queries was unbelievable. Wendy learned that their house at the top of their driveway was in Wilder, but their mailbox at the bottom of their driveway was in White River Junction. Her street and house number were still the same, but the town and zip code had changed back to White River Junction from Wilder, said the post office. You live where your mailbox is, not where your house is, they explained.

My mind rushed ahead to the next obvious question: If we were driving to Wendy and Bob's house, which address do we put in the GPS—her house address at the top of her driveway or her mailbox address at the bottom of her driveway?

A few clicks later I had my answer. When I entered her street address into my Google map app using Wilder VT as the town, it was automatically corrected to White River Junction, VT. Same street, same street number, but in White River Junction where her mailbox lives.

Wendy and Bob had officially moved from Wilder to White River Junction and never packed a box. Even moving is virtual now.

A GOOD NEWS DAY

As a child, if I wanted to talk with Dad, I figured that his car was a good place to chat, probably because he couldn't get away too easily.

So, one Monday morning when I was eleven years old, I jumped into the passenger's seat in Dad's car at about 8:00 AM and locked the doors. I wanted to be sure I got into the car before he did.

Dad was a salesman for a steel company, but all I knew as a child was that he sold pipes. I thought that meant he sold pipes door-to-door like the Fuller Brush man who went door-to-door selling household cleaning supplies. These were the only salesmen I knew about.

It turned out that besides selling corrugated steel pipes for carrying storm water, Dad also sold steel buildings to cities, counties, and the province. His job didn't sound at all interesting to a young girl like me. I always wished he had sold ice-cream like the Good Humor ice-cream man who rang his bell as he drove up the street. Ice-cream I could understand.

On this Monday morning I had something important to discuss with him, so I was getting a bit anxious. Suddenly Dad appeared, walking out of the house with his old brown briefcase towards his car. He smiled at me. I knew his smile wouldn't last long.

I had his car keys in my pocket, and I had locked all the doors from the inside, so he couldn't get in the car and go to work. *Sometimes heavy artillery is needed*, I reasoned. I was on a mission.

He pulled the door handle, and the door didn't open.

"What are you doing in there Diane? Unlock the door."

"Not until you say yes," I responded.

"Say yes to what?"

"You know." Jeepers, how could he not know? I had been talking about it for weeks.

"I want to get my ears pierced!" I shouted through the closed window. "It is my birthday in three weeks and that is all I want!" I continued pleading, "All the girls in my swim club have pierced ears." Not exactly "all" but I was directionally correct—*many* girls had pierced ears.

I could read his lips. "But you're younger than all of those girls," he countered. "Could you please unlock the door, so we don't have to yell through the glass?"

I unlocked his door, then he opened it and got into the driver's seat.

Continuing my rant, I said, "Dad, I'm always the youngest doing anything, so you shouldn't focus on my age. I know I'm just 11 but I'm president of my Grade 8 class—did you ever think about that?" Tears welled up in my eyes.

Then he said the words I was hoping to hear. "You've made a good case for getting your ears pierced, so Happy Birthday, Diane! Now get out of this car right now because I need to get to work so I can make money to buy you earrings!

There was more good news. Eight months later during the summer, he agreed to take me on a sales call to visit a customer two hours away in Windsor Ontario. It was similar to a "take your kids to work" day, but 30 years before it had become a school tradition. He even took me to lunch with his customer, Mr. Marentette, at a real grownup restaurant.

My dreams had all come true. I no longer felt like a kid—I had pierced ears, had been to a grown-up restaurant and had lunch with adults. Dad and I understood each other much better now, and I finally understood what corrugated steel pipe was.

THE BIRD DID IT

I thought I looked lovely that evening as we got ready to go out. I had delayed having my daily shower until an hour before we were leaving. As a result, my normally flat hair was still fluffy, and my freshly washed skin had a special glow that nobody but me could probably see. Some days it works, some days it doesn't, but I was really on my game that night, except for that little lipstick smudge on the edge of my lower lip.

We had a reservation for dinner on the outside deck of a restaurant with a group of friends. It was a perfect night—warm, clear, and not windy. Taking our seats, we ordered our meals which, for a few of us, included a creamy she-crab soup appetizer. My bowl of soup soon arrived, and those of us who ordered it dove into the delicious, steaming bowls of soup, figuratively speaking.

I soon became aware that I was shoveling the soup into my mouth at quite a pace—I just couldn't seem to get enough soup, fast enough. But when I looked down at my spoon, I realized it was a teaspoon, not a soup spoon like my friends had. With no server in sight, I continued my rapid-fire slurping from my little teaspoon.

Just as I was finishing my she-crab soup, I felt a big wet rain drop fall on my forehead. *Yikes, it's starting to rain, I thought.* I gazed upwards, but there were no clouds, no storms, and no rain.

Oh no.

I turned to my friend sitting beside me. "Linda, what colour is that wet spot on my face."

The look on her face told me what I feared. "It's white," she said with a grimace.

Oh no! It wasn't a rain drop at all! It was bird s**t!

A feathery perpetrator had dive bombed the table then fled after hitting its target—me. The only good news was that it had missed my fluffy, just-washed hair, so I still looked almost lovely except for the mess on my forehead. My table mates optimistically suggested that maybe I had missed my mouth given I was eating my she-crab soup at break-neck speed. I only wished that the splat was from soup.

After screeching "eeew," I then yelled to Honey at the far end of the table that a bird just s**t on my face. I can still hear all the husbands' laughing when they saw the mess. I excused myself to go the restroom to wash away the white splat.

As we were getting ready to leave the restaurant, Honey passed the check and his credit card to his seat mate saying, "Please pass this to Birds**t." I now understand how nick names get started.

The lesson we can all learn from that evening is to be sure to carry tissues in case a bird lays one on you. You can then quickly and discreetly wipe the bird poop off your face or other body part depending on the bird's aim.

Then—and this is always the hardest part for me—just shut up about it.

MEMORIES AND MISTAKES

My clearest memories about my life are from before I turned eight. Perhaps it's because my hard drive was nearly empty back then, or because everything that happened was brand new and exciting.

I painfully remember my mistakes, some of which were because the adults in my life took for granted that I understood how to do things when I had no clue.

Like most children, I was taught how to ride a bike, brush my teeth, and turn on the TV. I was even taught how to wash and dry the dinner dishes alongside my sister. I could pull weeds from the garden once Mom showed me the difference between a weed and a flower.

When I was in kindergarten, Mom put my clothes on a chair each morning for me to wear, as I couldn't yet be trusted to put together an outfit that didn't make me look like a clown. However, I seemed to have acquired some fashion sense by copying the way my Mom dressed me so that by first grade, I could dress for school on my own.

So how and where did I fall short? It was in the unscripted parts of life that rarely came up and where my common sense didn't guide me at all.

I clearly remember the black phone ringing one Saturday morning while Mom and Dad were still sleeping. Nobody had ever taught me how to answer it, so I picked up the ringing phone as I had seen Mom do and said hello. A man said to me, "Is your father home?"

"Yes, he is," I said, then promptly hung up the phone while I ran to get Dad. Please note—I didn't set the phone on the counter—I hung it up! Nobody had taught me what to do if the phone was for someone who wasn't standing beside me. When Dad came to the kitchen to get the phone, there it was, disconnected on the phone cradle. That was the last time I made that mistake. Mom, do you see how a little training might have helped?

But I made my biggest mistake on my sister Wendy's 3rd birthday. Mom was getting the cake and the decorations ready, but she still had some gifts that needed wrapping. This is where I came into the picture. She asked me to wrap a new dress for sister Wendy by rolling it in the wrapping paper, then tying it about 2 inches from each end with ribbon. Then I had to fringe the ends with the scissors so it would look frilly and festive for her birthday. I followed Mom's instructions and the gift looked gorgeous.

Or at least it did until my sister unwrapped it and discovered that when I fringed the ends with the scissors, I cut the dress into ribbons. Wendy's new party dress was hanging in shreds.

We four sisters didn't get new dresses often, so I knew that I had made a huge mistake. But I don't recall Mom yelling at me or sending me to my room, so I can only guess that she realized her instructions weren't clear enough for a 6-year-old and thus forgave me. But I never forgave myself for getting it so wrong.

The actions of my childhood became my memories as an adult, with all the wonder, pride, and sadness they have brought. I hope all my childhood memories stay with me well into old age, even when I reach the age where I struggle to get my kids' names right.

Life has a way of reversing itself over time, because now I must take care that my communication to my 93-year-old Mom is simple and clear. But even if Mom understands what I say, it doesn't mean she'll remember it for more than two minutes. But that's a whole other problem.

OUR FRUGAL TRIP
TO ITALY

During the last recession, my Love God and I were trying to live modestly. Then two airplane tickets complicated our lives.

I'm not expecting any sympathy when I tell you that we were forced to go on a trip to Italy because my Love God had two airline vouchers from Spumoni Airways when an earlier trip was cancelled. We had to use or lose the tickets before the end of September. Luckily, we had hundreds of reward points from having spent about three trillion dollars before the recession hit, so Honey booked five nights in hotels all over Italy.

My Love God's plan for our trip wasn't perfect though because he didn't have any reward points for *ristorante* food, which would have been useful if we planned to eat on our vacation. Instead, he suggested that I pack a week's worth of nutritious meals for overseas picnicking. He was picturing a box of Raisin Bran, a half-dozen bagels pre-spread with cream cheese, and some turkey wraps which would cover breakfast and lunch for seven days. Of course, we'd need to take a cooler complete with frozen cold packs which would cost us an extra one hundred dollars on Spumoni Airways due to our excess baggage. *Picnicking isn't cheap, Honey.*

My Love God had rented the smallest car available anywhere in Europe because—you guessed it— it was the cheapest. For the record, he is 6'2" tall and I am 6'2" wide so I wasn't sure that this was the car for us. We would need to tightly squeeze our cheeks to fit into this roller skate, but I figured we'd be fine once our nether regions were set free.

As for clothes, my Love God suggested that we pack lightly, and even recommended that if I reversed my underwear daily, one pair could last two days. Really. And given we didn't know anyone in Italy, nobody would care how bad we looked, he said, so I could skip taking my makeup bag and most of my clothes except for some underwear, a sweater and a pair of sweatpants. Sneakers would work best, he added, because we'd be climbing mountains and maybe we'd even yodel in Italian while we drank goat's milk in the Alps! Mamma Mia!

Our new modest lifestyle would not stop with our trip to Italy of course. My friend, Violette, who is French Canadian, suggested that Honey and I needed to adopt a life that was "simplicité voluntaire" during the recession. This is a popular approach to life for unemployed French people and even for Warren Buffett, who is not unemployed and not poor. But Warren has credibility with me because he has lived in the same three-bedroom house for over fifty years, which, although it shows he is dull also shows that he leads a voluntarily simple life quite happily. I suspect it's easier to live that way if you don't have to.

Money has never been at the core of my happiness. Having a beautiful sofa or a cashmere sweater has never brought me lasting happiness—okay, maybe a few moments of unadulterated joy—but in the space of life, stuff doesn't matter a hill of beans. A few laughs, lots of love and the occasional piece of good chocolate work for me.

BETTER THAN SEX

There were times when a seven-year-old girl simply had to take charge. I always hoped that Dad would think of going there on his own, but I couldn't take a chance.

"Dad, can we please go to Hansen's for an ice cream cone?" I would ask, gritting my little teeth as I waited for his response. If our entire family of six went to Hansen's, I knew that it would be an expensive outing—six cones at ten cents each would cost sixty cents. Perhaps Dad would think that was too much money— it was the fifties after all. But most often he'd say yes because he loved ice cream cones too.

There were other stores in our village that sold ice cream, but Hansen's was special. The ice cream freezer sat in the middle of the small drugstore like a showpiece. There was no soda counter in the tiny drugstore, just a few shelves of candy bars and potato chips.

The pharmacist, Mr. Hansen, scooped the cones himself, a task which didn't need his pharmaceutical education, but as a sole proprietor of the drugstore, he was called upon to wear many hats. His scoops of ice cream were very generous, but what I really loved was that Hansen's was the only store that had orange sherbet, my new favourite flavour. I had loved chocolate ice cream the most until I discovered orange sherbet.

Mr. Hansen also did something that was extra special—if you asked, he would dip your cone in a bowl of chocolate sprinkles. Orange sherbet cones covered in chocolate sprinkles fueled my lifelong passion for all treats combining orange and chocolate.

Years later, convenience stores sold a frozen confection called a "Jet," which was an orange sherbet bar covered in a layer of chocolate, but I haven't found a Jet bar anywhere in thirty years so they must have stopped making them.

On our Caribbean cruise honeymoon in 1991, I spotted an ice cream stand on the deck of the pool where Honey and I were lounging, so I snuck away to see what flavors they had. My eyes anxiously searched through the tubs of ice cream lined up in the freezer, until I hit the jackpot—orange sherbet! And as if that weren't fabulous enough, they also had chocolate sprinkles. Hallelujah!

As I sat with Honey enjoying my cone, I confessed to him that *sometimes* I would even choose orange sherbet with chocolate sprinkles over sex, a perhaps unwise admission on our honeymoon. But luckily it turned out I could have both, no choosing required, even thirty years later.

CAN YOU MOVE IT?

Whump!

Our youngest son's rollerbladed feet shot straight out from under him on the driveway. His screech could have raised the dead as he landed heavily on his arm. I knew it would be just a matter of time before those roller skates betrayed him, causing bodily injury.

He raised his arm limply in front of me as he winced. The arm looked normal to me. "Can you move it?" I questioned, in my best nurse voice.

He nodded.

"Then you must have just bruised it—let's get some ice on it." No need to dwell on every childhood ache and pain, right?

The next morning before summer camp, he complained that his arm was sore and maybe he shouldn't go to camp.

"Can you move it?" I asked again, just to double check that my diagnostic skills were intact. He nodded. "Then you're fine. Off to camp now."

My office phone rang at 2:00 p.m. It was the camp counsellor.

"Your son just tripped over a tree root and fell on his sore arm. He says it hurts."

Jeepers…can that boy not stay on his feet for just one day? Is he determined to torment me? I packed up some of my office work and headed for camp.

His Royal Shortness was sitting on a log, rubbing the offending arm. "It feels much better now, Mom," he said as I reflected on all the work I'd just left behind at the office to tend to an arm that felt much better.

"Can you move it?" I inquired, asking the only medical question I knew to ask in such circumstances. He nodded. "Well, good. It's fine then."

"Do you think I should play in the soccer game tonight?" he wondered.

"Of course," I replied, sensing the start of a pity party. "You can't let your team down just because your arm is a bit sore. A little pain never hurt anybody, son."

I continued lecturing as only a mother can, hoping to teach him the importance of biting the bullet, sucking it up, and all the other metaphors meant to make men out of boys. *That's my job, right?*

The game warm up began with our man-boy goalie in place, stopping each ball with his left arm, while the impaired right arm lay limply at his side. I admit it looked kind of peculiar.

Just as I was pondering this odd-looking scene, a soccer ball missile hit his dangling right arm. That would be the same arm that he had assured Nurse Mom he could move and that I had assured him was fine.

My Love God, who had remained silent on my medical diagnostic technique to that point, said impatiently, "Do you *think* you could take him to the hospital to have it checked?"

Jeepers! Did my Love God grow up under a mushroom? Did he not receive the same medical education from his parents that I had—that if an arm can move, it can't possibly be broken? Are we raising a marshmallow or a man-to-be? Is no one listening? The boy can move it! He said so himself!

By then it was clear that I'd need to prove the soundness of my medical advice with a four-hour wait in the emergency room. We sat and sat. They finally X-rayed the limb, which had been sitting like a wet noodle on his lap.

"What do you think is wrong, Mom?"

Testing one last time that it really was a moveable limb, I asked, "Can you move it?" He nodded. I felt like I had been singing a refrain from a familiar song. "Then it's just a bad bruise, son."

The doctor appeared. "Mrs. Pascoe, your son has a broken arm and will need a cast on it for six weeks." His words pierced my heart.

"WHAAAT?" I croaked. "But he can move it—isn't that the rule?"

Was my medical training flawed? Would child services be called and sentence me to baking brownies for the little man-boy whenever his stomach rumbled?

"Son, I am so sorry," I apologized. "I didn't know. Can you ever forgive me?"

"Sure, Mom—but can you please carry my backpack, shoes, coat, and books for me? I know it's heavy, but a little pain never hurt anybody."

Ouch.

STRANGER DANGER

One day when I was nine, I stayed home from school because I had a sore throat. My mother had gone shopping for a few groceries, leaving me with my two younger sisters for a short time. Suddenly I heard a loud noise at the door. KNOCK! KNOCK! KNOCK! I went to answer it.

A man was delivering some clothes from a children's store called "Young Canada."

"Is your mother home?" the delivery man asked.

"No, she went to the store," I told him truthfully. I know, I know, but it was the 50's.

He paused. "Can I use your bathroom before I leave?" he asked. *When a guy's got to go, he's got to go, right?*

"Okay," I said as he entered the house. I lead him to the bathroom and went back to wait in the family room. He soon reappeared and said, "Would you mind if I used the phone to call the store?"

Made sense to 9-year-old me. "Okay," I responded and showed him to the phone. He picked it up but didn't dial it. He wrote something on a piece of paper, then said, "It's okay. I'll talk to my boss when I get back to the store."

He walked out the door and out of my life.

Well, not quite.

A short time later, the phone rang, and a man asked me if I knew where babies came from. I hung up. I knew it was the delivery man. When Mom came home, I told her what had happened, and she called the store to report him. I became much less trusting after that, which was clearly a good thing.

Eight years later I walked to the main road a block away from my house to catch a ride to school with my friend, but my friend was sick that day, and didn't show up. I walked back home, and Mom said she would drive me. As I waited for her to get ready, the phone rang. A man who sounded like he had a mouth full of marbles started to talk dirty and I hung up fast. Can't trick this girl twice.

I told Mom I thought it was the strange man who lived in a house I passed every day on my way to meet my friend for a ride. He would have seen me walk back home. Later that year, a young girl I used to see on my bus line was found murdered about a half mile from our house. He was charged with the murder but ultimately not convicted. No one was, but I have always felt deep down that it was him. I could have been that girl.

Many years later when I was 35, I was living on the second floor of a house in Toronto when I heard the doorbell ring. I ran down the stairs, partially opening the windowless door to see a tall man with a scruffy beard standing there.

"I'm looking for my friend who lives in this area and wondered if I could use your phone to ask him what his address is?" he said.

My brain screamed *stranger danger.* I was no longer the naïve girl who once allowed the delivery man into the house.

"If you give me his phone number, I can call him to get his address for you," I offered.

He paused, then said "No, it's all right" and walked away. It felt like a close call.

Fortunately, I was not harmed in any of these incidents but as a result of these experiences, I became wiser and more cautious. Three moments with strangers. Three times I could have been a murder victim on *Forensic Files.*

That's not exactly how I'd like to make my TV debut.

I'M TELLING ON YOU

Life was vastly different and much safer back in the early sixties.

I was only nine years old, but Mom said I could take the London city bus all by myself to my swimming lessons that week. To be clear, it's not the London where the Queen lives, but the London near Toronto, a big city where many of our relatives lived.

Grabbing my swim bag from the kitchen table, I checked to be sure I had two pink bus tickets in my wallet, then started running across the neighbour's lawn to get to the bus stop. Luckily, we only lived a block away from the end of the bus line where it turned around and headed back to town, so I could catch the bus coming or going.

Halfway to the bus stop, I heard a voice behind me. Out of the corner of my eye, I saw my youngest sister running after me, crying.

"I come too!" she screamed.

"No, no, no! Go home right now, Elaine. You can't come with me! I'm going swimming." She didn't care what I said—she kept running towards me.

I tried again. "You're going to be in really big trouble if I tell Mom and Dad about this!" I used the ultimate threat to see if that made her turnaround. I desperately wished I were an only child—having three sisters always made life complicated. It also made it hard to feel special when there was a herd of us to consider.

"I come!" she wailed again, ignoring my threat. "I swim too."

Elaine continued to run towards me, arms flailing and tears dripping down her face. I started to cry too. If I kept running to catch the bus, she'd follow me, ending up a block away from home on a busy street where she'd get run over and end up dead. Then *I'd* be the one in big trouble with Mom and Dad.

But if I had to take that screaming kid back home, I'd miss the bus, my swimming lesson, probably fail the course and not get my swimming certificate.

Why didn't Mom just tie her to the backyard clothes-line so she couldn't escape from the house or lock that kid in her bedroom for a year or two.

Suddenly, I heard a different voice calling my name. *Who is yelling at me now? Why doesn't everyone just leave me alone?* I thought.

I looked up and saw a neighbour on her porch.

"Do you need help, Diane?" she asked.

"My sister keeps following me—I'm going to miss my bus and my swimming lesson because I have to take her home. I'm so mad at her! "

The lady ran over to Elaine then scooped her up in her arms. "I'll take her back to your house, but you need to run to catch your bus — I just saw it go by. It'll come back to your bus stop in about three minutes."

"Oh, thank you very much!" I yelled to the lady as I started running. I made it to the bus stop with a minute to spare.

But the week was different for this young girl in another way. Besides allowing me to take the bus by myself every day that week, Mom also did something incredibly special and unheard of—she put five dimes in my wallet with a note saying I could buy myself an ice cream cone every day after my swimming lesson!

See, I really was special! Sisters, eat your hearts out.

MY CHECKERED LIFE

Last Saturday I needed to make a quick stop at the grocery store for some boneless, skinless chicken thighs. As I always do when I go into a store, I wore one of the fabric masks that my neighbour, Linda, made for me.

My mask that day was made from a fabric in black and white houndstooth, a favourite pattern. She has also made me a fabric mask covered in red lipstick kisses because I'm also crazy about red lipstick. These masks perfectly reflect my fashion obsessions. Even if my friends and acquaintances can't see my face, they may recognize my roundish body and grey hair, but mostly they recognize my signature masks.

If someone comments on my lipstick mask, it's the perfect conversation starter for me to mention my first book, *Life Isn't Perfect but My Lipstick Is*. Next thing I know my business cards are flying out of my purse and landing in the unsuspecting person's hand. A week later when I'm checking my book's sales on Amazon, another book or two has popped onto my sales report.

But my houndstooth fabric mask is a different story because it's unrelated to the theme of either of my books and therefore it isn't a natural conversation starter. Until this week, when a woman cruising down the aisle near the chicken thighs, stopped and stared at me. Even with her mask and glasses on, I could see her eyes bulging. Did she want to know how I planned to cook my chicken thighs perhaps? Was I blocking the aisle? It is never easy to read the emotions of mask wearers whose faces are mostly hidden.

Then she spoke to me loudly and clearly. "Is this intentional or is it just a happening?" the woman asked, eyes crinkled and her finger pointing at my clothes.

I looked down at myself and suddenly it all made sense. In addition to my black and white houndstooth mask, I was also wearing a houndstooth shirt, houndstooth shoes and was carrying a houndstooth bag. Good thing I wasn't wearing my houndstooth leggings, nor any of my nine houndstooth scarves or shawls, or I would have looked like someone had wallpapered me with houndstooth.

I burst into laughter and assured her I knew my fabric preferences were unusual and limited— I wear what I like and apparently, I like houndstooth, big buffalo checks and all other black and white checks including gingham, which is a sub-species of houndstooth.

But my new friend near the chicken thighs at Lowe's knew I was a fashion faux pas as soon as she saw me: a bit of checkered clothing is nice but wearing top-to-toe checks is over the top.

When I stand in front of our black and white buffalo check curtains in our family room wearing my houndstooth bath robe and slippers, I am invisible except for my face and hair. Some have used the word obsessive to describe me. Ok, maybe a wee bit.

I recently found a picture of me taken thirty years ago wearing a houndstooth sweater, so clearly nothing has changed. Black and white gingham check fabrics have been in my wardrobe since elementary school, so I'm quite sure that my mother created this monster.

People much more famous than I also have checkered wardrobes, I learned recently when a friend gave me a magazine describing the current rage for checks and houndstooth patterned fabrics. In one photo, Queen Elizabeth was wearing a houndstooth suit. Yup. Is it a coincidence that we like the same fabric? I think not. Queenie and I may even be related as her last name and my maiden name are Windsor, so it may be that my love of houndstooth and other checks is in my genes.

The genetic roots of my checkered fabric obsession were further evident this week when my sister sent me a large box of my elderly Mom's scarves and wraps. Yup - all black and white checks and houndstooth fabrics.

This confirms that it's a DNA issue with no known cure, so please let me be.

THE JEEP

Santa's Christmas gifts to our kids were like the academy awards—we needed a Best Gift and then a few Best Supporting Gifts. The Best Gift from Santa to our youngest son in 1996 was a bicycle that he could ride to school and to visit his friends in the neighbourhood. We were sure he would be extremely excited and surprised because he hadn't asked for it.

Before Christmas, Santa usually hid the gifts under the bed in the guest room, in the trunks of our cars, and in other places too high for kids to reach or to see, requiring parental gymnastics to hide the gifts. We were very clever about our hiding spots, we thought, even storing gifts at our elderly neighbour's house.

Santa's Best Supporting Gifts for our boy would fill the space under the tree. Santa was going to bring him a big yellow toy crane, a baseball glove, new hockey skates, the annual new hockey stick as well as various DVDs and games.

Santa didn't wrap his gifts, but the gifts from parents were always wrapped in Christmas paper, and were usually practical gifts like clothes, underwear, socks, or pajamas. Ho hum.

As Christmas drew near, our youngest son was pouring through the store flyers, pausing to look at an expensive battery-operated Jeep, the Rolls Royce of transportation for a five-year-old boy. Jeeps came up from time to time in conversations that December though I tried to discourage Honey from such talk to remove any youthful expectations.

Christmas morning arrived, and as was the rule, our boy couldn't go downstairs to the Christmas tree until he woke us up, and never before 6 AM. That way, we could enjoy his excitement when he saw his gifts.

The boy bounded into our bedroom at 6:15 AM, yelling at us that it was time to get up. We all headed to the living room where unwrapped gifts from Santa and wrapped gifts from us lay sprawled around.

Then came the moment that neither Honey nor I wanted to hear.

"Where's my Jeep?" our son cried as we stared at the bicycle where our son had pictured a Jeep.

Honey and I looked at each other, horrified. This wasn't the way it was supposed to go. *See, I told you, Honey!*

I sputtered the only thing I could think to stay. "I guess Santa thought a bike would be more fun for you. He's a smart man. He probably knew you would like to go bike riding with your siblings and your friends."

The silence was deafening as my words hung in the air.

Quietly he uttered, "I guess you're right." He pulled himself up on the bicycle, pumping the pedals to make the wheels spin. A smile crept onto his face as he experienced the thrill of a bike for the first time, but it would be even more fun when he was on the road.

The exploration and unwrapping continued for another hour as we all expressed our joy and thanks for our wonderful gifts. As we stuffed the wrapping paper and ribbons into the garbage bag, our son hesitantly said, "But where are the gifts that were hidden under the bed in the guest room?"

Whoa! That boy had really cased the joint. Those presents would have remained under the bed until next Christmas, if he hadn't searched everywhere in the house for his gifts and then reminded his forgetful parents that they had missed putting out some gifts.

So much for great hiding spots.

FAT LIES

I had just announced to my Love God that I was going to join that famous weight-loss program for my second go-around. You know, the triumph of hope over experience. My lost weight had crept back, as it often has. So, it was time to sign up again, pay my monthly dues, and waddle into the weekly meetings.

I went to my first meeting, version 2.0, and weighed in. I cringed as I saw my weight recorded in the weigh-in record book. How did it get to this, I wondered? The last time I weighed myself, I weighed far less. Well, OK, that *was* two years ago. Time flies, and fat returns when you aren't paying attention.

With a straight face, my Love God then asked the forbidden question: "So what do you weigh?"—as if that were a normal marital question, like "Have you seen my sunglasses, dear?"

Did I hear that man correctly? Has he learned nothing after thirty years with me and fourteen with his first wife?

OK, fine—if he insisted on asking a dumb question, I'd give him a dumb answer.

"I weigh one hundred and fourteen pounds," I replied, looking him straight in the eye. That ought to stop him in his tracks. Let him prove I'm wrong. Silly man.

"One hundred and fourteen—really?" he said, eyebrows raised. "That's very interesting."

I'd lied, and we both knew it. Let the games begin.

I wanted to dress as lightly as possible for my second weigh-in a week later, so I took my kitchen food scales into the bathroom to weigh various bras and panties. As I was leaving the bathroom, I was startled to meet my Love God in the doorway. He'd been watching me. I was like a deer caught in the headlights.

"What in heaven's name are you doing?" he asked.

I was tempted to lie again but braved the truth.

"I was weighing my underwear to see which pieces weighed the least."

He rolled his eyes and shook his head, trying to ignore this Lucy moment.

When I arrived home from the meeting, my Love God was waiting for me. "So how did the meeting go?" he asked. In Honey-speak that meant, "Did you lose any weight?"

"The meeting went well—I was down two and a half pounds."

"So, what do you weigh now?"

Jeepers, did he think I was a mathematician? *Lying is so complicated,* I thought. I had to quickly recalculate my fake weight, subtracting two and a half pounds from 114 pounds with him staring at me. My weigh-in record book told the truth, but this conversation was not about the truth.

This is the way it has gone for six months. Honey asks every week what my new weight is. I recalibrate my fake weight to correspond with my true weight loss. Apparently, I now weigh eighty-seven pounds, with a final goal weight of sixty-four pounds.

Oh, what a tangled web we weave...

FANCY PANTS

"You should always wear clean underwear because you never know if you'll have to go to the hospital."

My mother's advice has echoed in my head for more than sixty years. I seriously doubt that the hospital staff stand around the nurses' station chatting about the sorry condition of their patients' underwear, but I can't take a chance. I have changed them every day exactly as Mom told me to do.

I usually buy three packs of underwear at a time, each pack holding six pairs of white cotton briefs so that my drawer is always full of clean panties. They're not that pretty, but they're functional, much like me.

When I'm at the hospital having scans, MRI's, mammograms, or x-rays, I never know when I might need to leave my undies on and when I might need to take them off. It seems that some imaging processes can handle panties but not bras because of their metal underwires, clasps and hooks. For some other tests, you need to be in your birthday suit under your hospital robe.

On a recent hospital visit, I was asked to leave my panties on for a needle biopsy in my back. As I lay there thinking about my exposed cotton underwear, I was wondering if the medical folks thought they were a tad plain, so I made a mental note to up my underwear game.

Two weeks later, I was back at the hospital for another scan, still wrestling with that troublesome hospital robe. Once again, I worried about whether my briefs needed to be on or off until the nurse assured me that they had to go.

Thank goodness I hadn't spent any money buying those fancy new undies covered with red lipstick motifs that I had found online, though they would have been quite a conversation piece under those bright lights.

Whoa! A great marketing idea came to me in a flash. As a way of promoting my first book, I could custom order some undies with an imprint of my book cover, *Life Isn't Perfect but My Lipstick Is*, displayed on the backside that only my medical team and Honey would see. The doctors and nurses might be prompted to buy a book or two out of curiosity or they might author a story about me and my unique undies for the hospital newsletter.

I wish Mom could see me in the hospital in those undies.

THE FURRY SCURRY

I was dog-tired and it was my son's fault. If he had done as I taught him and brought me flowers or chocolates for Mother's Day like any normal son, I would not have been laid up on the sofa, unable to move a muscle.

But no—he had to think for himself and be different on Mother's Day. He had the nerve to pay the entry fee for me and our two dogs to go in a four-mile walk called the "Furry Scurry" in support of a local dog charity. However noble the scurry was, it sounded like work for me, the dogs, and for my Love God whom I recruited to walk with us. Given I'm not furry and I rarely scurry, I would have been more than willing to write the charity a check then park myself in front of the TV watching my favourite forensic murder shows. But this was not to be—he paid for us to walk, so walk we would.

The day of the Furry Scurry arrived. We drove for an hour and a half, arriving at the starting gate hot to trot. Wyatt the Lab and Carley the Wiener Dog were yanking on their leashes, eager to absorb all the new smells along the walking path.

We stationed ourselves at the back of the pack, knowing that Carley, with her short sausage legs, would be in everyone's way. There were dogs and owners in every shape and size who were making their way along the sandy path which meandered through the fields. Luckily, there were occasional trees and bushes which offered much needed shade, and the organizers supplied bowls of water for the dogs to drink. One exhausted border collie, lying off to the side of the path, took advantage of his water break to have a little nap in the shade. Wouldn't I have loved to do that too.

Up hills and down hills in the scorching sun or cooling shade we went. Carley's short legs, moving non-stop, needed regular shade breaks for relief from the hot sand. Wyatt, with his long legs, cruised along the path, enabling him to outpace smaller dogs, but he too was tired as we neared the end of the four-mile furry scurry. We crossed the finish line, exhausted, yet proud of our accomplishment.

All the furry scurriers were crowded around big tubs of water at the finish line, trying to get a slurp of water. Carley, too short for her head to reach the water, had to be lifted into a water tub to get a drink. Before we headed for home, our weary duo gobbled treats of various sorts as a reward for a walk well done.

When we arrived home, I lay on the sofa, legs stretched out, exhausted. I put an ice pack on my right heel to numb the pain. There was sand buried under my toenails and embedded in my cracked heels, while my hair was stiff from the sweat and dust that mixed together into a sticky mess. The dogs lay spread eagle, snoring on the rug, while Honey fell asleep sitting up in his big chair, mouth open. We were all zonked.

The furry scurry was the start of something great as it turned out. The four of us signed up for three more charity walks that year, but luckily none were on field trails covered with hot sand.

On another happy note, our son dropped by to see us, bringing chocolates and a card for Mother's Day, just as I had taught him. Sweat and sweets—a perfect gift combination for Mother's Day.

WE COULD NEVER FORGET

Our lives go in stages and my mother has now moved into the next, and possibly last, stage of her life. No longer able to live safely at home, she moved into a nursing home about a mile up the road from her house. Her days involve lying in her bed watching TV or wheeling around in her wheelchair in the common room.

Still skinny, still witty, still funny. Still sleeps most of the time. All that time spent lying in bed has created a new problem. Mom's wispy white hair gets tangled in a knot on the back of her head because her hair constantly rubs against the pillowcase. Trying to untangle it gets the same screeches from her as it would from a toddler, but a quick spray of detangler softens the mess so it can be brushed. Another crisis is averted.

Mom announced in late January that she was going to leave her three-foot-tall Santa Claus on her side table all year long because she loves it. Santa seemed fine with it, and the nurses and my sisters didn't much care— whatever worked for Mom.

The staff genuinely adore Mom. She's engaging, jokes around, and even sticks her tongue out at them playfully. She looks like the Easter bunny because all her clothes and slippers are made of fluffy fabric to keep her warm. Sitting in a wheelchair during the day, she's usually covered in a large Sherpa blanket with a furry muff on her lap to keep her cold hands warm. She is quite a sight.

She chats mostly to family and staff. "Have a good day Carol," a nurse said.

Mom responded, "We'll see. I'll get back to you later on that."

Some days are better than others, of course, but she comes around with a bit of conversation and love. Our phone conversations are recycled, as neither of us can recall what we chatted about on earlier calls, and with not too much happening in her life, it's hard to find scintillating things to talk about.

But last Monday was a difficult day. She didn't want a shower she told the nurse, wrapping her arms around the nurse to punctuate her refusal. She didn't want her meds either—tasted bad, she grouched. Nor did she want to talk to her daughters, she declared defiantly, even though she loves talking to us all. As she walked past a man asleep in a chair in the TV room, she yelled, "I saw you kill her!" referring to his wife. Yikes! Luckily, Mom can zoom to the moon but returns to earth just as quickly.

The following day, the nurse who was trying to give Mom her meds tried a new approach. She cajoled her with an offer that she knew Mom couldn't refuse. The nurse had a huge bust which had always fascinated Mom, who is flat as a pancake. But when the nurse told Mom she could put her hand in her deep cleavage if she took her meds, Mom was giddy with excitement, and swallowed her meds without any fuss then buried her hand in the nurse's cleavage for a feel. The nurse and Mom both think their little game is funny.

So, here's the background story on Mom and her boobs: Mom was never fat in her younger years because she ate so little, preferring to have a cigarette rather than food back in the day. She rarely weighed much more than 100 pounds, so she never had the fat needed to grow her own boobs. Her A cup brassieres were usually stuffed with Kleenex to fill them out under a sweater or blouse, so her infatuation with boobs as an almost 93-year-old is easily traceable to her younger years. But she's alert enough to know that talk of boobs is funny and harmless.

On our next phone call, I asked Mom if she had been given her vaccination yet for COVID-19.

"That sounds familiar," she said.

"Is one of your upper arms sore?" She felt both arms.

"Yes, my left arm is a bit sore. Now that I think about it, I do remember getting a needle. What is COVID-19 anyway?" she asked me for the umpteenth time, prompting a meaningful conversation about the COVID 19 virus that she understands in the moment, but forgets by the time we have our next chat or maybe even within ten minutes.

We remind Mom in every conversation how much we love her and think about her. She says she loves to hear that and to know we haven't forgotten her. Don't worry Mom. We could never forget.

THE SQUARE DANCE

For over sixty years I have wondered why I was selected to be a square dancer with three other girls and four boys, all in grade two or three.

I was not an obvious choice. The other three girls, cute with long flowing hair, took dance lessons after school. I wasn't so cute—my poker straight bangs were cut on an angle an inch above my eyebrows. One of my front baby teeth was chipped, or had possibly decayed, leaving me with an enthusiastic but flawed smile.

I wasn't a dancer nor was I graceful, but I wasn't completely without talent. I had won the long jump contest and bicycle obstacle race for six and seven-year-old girls only a month earlier, but I doubt that such talent would have flagged me for being an excellent square dancer.

But all four girls had one thing in common — we were all good students. The boys—not so much. The reason for the boys having been chosen is still unclear—some were tall, some short, some skinny, some husky, but I would bet that these boys were chosen because they lived close to the school and could get to our lunch hour practices on time.

The best part of being a square dancer was having a new dress sewn by my mother. It was unlike any dress I owned — it was an orange-colored dress with a big circle skirt supported by a crinoline which gave the dress a fancy look when I twirled onstage. A black sash covered in orange, green and yellow flowers was tied at my waist, while a white Peter Pan collar around the neck of the dress set off my round face.

Every lunch hour we practiced our square dance routine to get ready for the citywide competition at the fairgrounds in late September. I wasn't that great at following sequences of steps, not just in dancing but later in cheerleading, or now that I think about it, following instructions in general. But I tried hard, I really did.

My dancing partner was Jimmy Watson, a grade two classmate with a large scar on his forearm. I could tell that he didn't like holding hands or touching me in any way while we were dancing, but there was no way around it. He never once spoke to me during our practices.

The night of the square dance competition at the Western Fair finally arrived. I was extremely excited but mostly because I thought I looked beautiful in my new dress. We performed our routine on stage just as we had practiced every day.

Or we did until I shut my eyes and twirled as I enjoyed the crowd's attention. When I opened my eyes, I was nowhere near Jimmy and had to dart back across the stage to join my mute partner. But it was too late—the damage was done. We were no longer in a square.

We didn't win the competition that night, but the pain of losing was lessened for me by my joy in having the best new dress ever.

This experience taught me something important: It's fine to twirl in life but don't overdo it and lose your way. Focus on what you are trying to do, do it well and *then* you can twirl as much as you like.

SAVE THE DATE

During a TV interview, the famous actor said that the main fear he had in life was that no one would show up to his funeral. Not that he would ever know, of course, but it got me thinking about solutions to his problem, even though I can assure you he has nothing to worry about.

The first thing I would suggest he do would be to send a "save the date" notice to people he would like to attend his funeral, just as people do for weddings. Of course, the date would be TBA, but it would put people on notice that he would be pleased if they would attend.

Then, when he died, his spouse could send out real invitations to those who received a "save the date" card. His spouse could even offer food at the funeral like chocolate chip cookies, or chocolate kisses and maybe add a door prize. Maybe the funeral director could even be playing the deceased's best movies during his funeral.

If the celebrity becomes ill and death is near, he could put an announcement on Facebook suggesting that readers stay tuned for another final announcement, encouraging them to attend his funeral. In truth, his funeral could fill a football stadium, so he might want to hire a publicist to ensure that his funeral date and time is broadcast widely so lots and lots of people will attend. Then he could rest in peace while alive, knowing many people would show up.

I have given a bit thought to what should happen when I pass away. I am not concerned about a traditional funeral as I don't want one, but a party thrown by Honey and Carley the Wiener Dog, wearing her best sweater, would be perfect. Lots of food and wine ought to ensure that a few people attend. Honey can read his favourite essays of the ones that I have written and hopefully he'd wear his shirt covered in dachshund cartoons. But with all the things to worry about before I die, wondering who will attend my event is the least of them.

Sorry, Mr. Celebrity, you need to find something useful to worry about in your life.

I MUST BE A GENIUS

Two weeks ago, Honey and I threw a "Costco dinner" at our home for six neighbors after a day of golf. The day before we had gone to Costco and bought wine, crackers and cheese, salads, rolls, chicken potpie, shepherd's pie, and key lime pie—a meal of pies really. It was a heat-and-eat meal which kept preparation at a minimum and fun at a maximum. No mixing, stirring, layering, or following recipes. Easy yet tasty.

I was really onto something, I figured, so we invited some other friends over for a Costco prepared meal a week later. My only extra effort for this meal was to toast the salad croutons in a pan on the stove top—so much tastier than plain cardboard croutons. I heated up the pan, then added olive oil, the croutons, and a few seasonings.

I heard Honey talking to our neighbour in the garage, so standing in the doorway, we exchanged pleasantries. I then noticed a friend out on the sidewalk motioning to me to come out to see her, which I did.

Two minutes later I heard Honey yell to me and our neighbour, "Can anyone besides me hear a car alarm going off somewhere?"

"I don't hear any car alarm, Honey, but I can faintly hear a sound coming from the direction of the house."

Our neighbour frowned then asked me, "Do you have something on the stove or in the oven?"

"I don't think so," I said pensively. *Hmmm, what had I been doing in the house before I came outside?* Good gawd! I had been toasting croutons in a pan on the stove!

I ran into the house, with Honey and our neighbour in hot pursuit, only to be overwhelmed by the smoke from burned croutons, four screeching smoke alarms and a disembodied voice yelling to any inhabitants to get out because there was a fire!

Our two scared dogs had tried to escape—the wiener dog was cowering near the front door and the yellow Lab had fled to the far end of the screened porch to avoid the shrieking alarms.

Honey silenced one smoke alarm after the other, putting new batteries in the smoke alarms while he was at it. I opened all the doors and windows to let the smoke clear. The frying pan was badly charred, so I trashed the evidence quickly.

Leaving croutons toasting and not remembering was a sure sign I was getting old. In the future, I vowed, I would stay in the house whenever I was baking.

Right.

The next week, while Honey had a snooze after his golf game, I baked a batch of chocolate chip cookies, setting the timer for twelve minutes. Then I took the wiener dog out for a pee and a poop, when I suddenly remembered that I had cookies baking! Luckily, the timer woke Honey up and he rescued the batch of cookies before they were cremated, happily wolfing down three cookies as his reward.

It's an understatement to say I'm not learning from my mistakes. I forget what I'm doing within three minutes of swearing that I won't forget.

Maybe I need to buy the special motion detector for the stove that I saw online. If I don't move at least once every five minutes, say the instructions, then the stove will shut off entirely. This would mean that I must dance or jump up and down while I cook to avoid the oven shutting off all while our meal is still cooking. Heck, I might even be able to lose a pound or two if I move enough.

Of course, finding a solution for the safe operation of the oven assumes that I will remember to turn the oven on in the first place. Yup, I've forgotten to do that before as well. Dinner was delayed by almost an hour that evening.

According to science, being forgetful is a sign of intelligence.

I must be a genius.

LESS STYLE, MORE SUBSTANCE

When I heard the results of our former US President's last physical exam, I realized we have our priorities wrong. We need to care a bit less if Presidents are fat and a lot more if they are honest, smart, trustworthy, self-aware, able to work well with others, and have a commitment to public service, not personal gain. And we need to know these things *before* candidates run for the Top Dog job

The way it works now, any John, Dick or Harriet can run for the top leadership job if they meet three basic criteria: they must be born in the US, have been a resident for at least 14 years, and be at least 35 years old. A lot of goofs can slip into the candidate pool by meeting such minimal requirements. I aim to change this for the 2024 election but there might need to be an amendment to the constitution for me to launch my plan to cut unsuitable candidates, so I need to get started now.

Just to be clear, policies and politics will not be my concern. The public will have to judge the candidate's opinions on these matters with the help of the press and media whose tenacity in probing everything about a candidate in televised interviews is well known.

We need to have a process to decide a potential candidate's mental fitness and leadership suitability. The voting public can't always know for certain if a candidate has mental health issues or character flaws that make them seriously unsuited to lead the country. We don't need any more keeners showing up at the party's primary debates to dazzle the public with their blustering rhetoric. We need less style, more substance,

Here's the best part—I'm volunteering to handle this employment testing for free. Well okay, not exactly free. I would need a supply of dark chocolate kisses, some Mr. Big chocolate bars and salted caramel ice cream to keep me motivated. I know it'll take a lot of time, but it'll be worth temporarily giving up my book club and golf games if I can get this right.

First, I would put together a valid job profile of the attributes the Top Dog must have. Good looks won't count nor will wealth.

Next, candidates from all parties interested in the leadership job will send their applications directly to me, and I will put them through a battery of HR employment tests that have been specifically designed to assess candidates against the mental and personality requirements to be a successful President.

I would conduct cognitive tests to measure a candidate's intellectual capability. We only want people running for the Top Dog position if they're smart, not just smooth talkers. Narcissists, sociopaths, and psychopaths need not apply.

I would also do personality tests to assess how the candidate wannabes manage conflict, make decisions, their aptitude for thinking, and their emotional intelligence. These tests would determine their ability to work well with colleagues, interact with the public, and handle disappointments and frustrations in a mature and professional way. Wouldn't that be nice.

Each candidate would also need to submit a reference letter from their kindergarten teacher as not much changes after kindergarten. If the teacher has passed away, I'd accept the candidate's year-end report card where the teacher comments on their abilities to cooperate, play well with others, focus on their work, share with others, and say sorry if they hurt other people. No bullies will be considered. Being described as "bright" or "curious" would be a significant plus.

Candidates in any party can only run in the primaries if they pass my tests and kindergarten reference check. Might as well weed out the misfits early and not waste everyone's time. This could reduce the field of candidates considerably but at least the ones who pass will be mentally fit for the Top Dog position.

The Presidential wannabes who pass my criteria would then be let loose on the public to campaign. The ones who flunk my tests and reference checks can go back to their old jobs and I'll never blab to the public about their shortfalls for the Top Dog job.

Physicians can still do those optional physical exams to figure out if a President or candidate has progressed from fat to obese, or if their ticker has issues or if their blood pressure is sky high. Such below-the-neck assessments are mainly done for public relations reasons, but I want testing above the neck to ensure that all candidates fit the requirements to lead the country.

Bring on my salted caramel ice-cream and dark chocolate kisses!

ACKNOWLEDGEMENTS

There are a few people I would like to recognize as contributors to this book. I would not have any stories to tell if it were not for the good humour of my husband, kids, friends, neighbors, sisters and Mom. Thank you for allowing me to include your lives in my essays.

Thank you also to my writing group, the Writers of the Forest, in Brunswick Forest, Leland, NC, for their patience and encouragement, as well as for the joy they bring me when they read their prose and poetry every week.

Thank you so much to my talented niece Meredith Durkee for her front cover illustration which suits me perfectly.

I would also like to tell my readers how much I truly appreciate them. They make it all worthwhile.

ABOUT THE AUTHOR

Diane Pascoe is from London, Ontario where she attended elementary school, high school, and Western University. She later graduated in business from York University. In 2004 Diane moved to North Carolina with her husband and their youngest son. She worked as a career professional in Human Resources in Toronto, Canada and in the Raleigh, NC area.

They recently retired near Wilmington NC where the weather is warm, the beach is nearby, and local golf courses encourage year-round golfing. Their last vacation trip was to South Africa in February 2020, just before the pandemic changed the world. Timing is everything.

When Diane retired, she published her real-life humour essays in her first book, *Life Isn't Perfect but My Lipstick Is*. She continued to write her essays which were then collected in her second humour essay book, *Never Argue with a Wiener Dog: You'll Lose*.

Where I'm From

I'm from a place where people are friendly yet reserved and love to laugh at themselves, as individuals and as Canadians.

I'm from a two-story house with a basement, and a swimming pool surrounded by a patio covered in outdoor carpet, in the suburbs of London, Ontario in the Land of Eh, where it is frosty cold on winter days.

I'm from pine, maple, and oak trees, and from the land of lakes where cottages dot the water's edge, and where ice cream cones are mandatory on hot summer days.

I'm from a place where you are polite to others, conserve the land, do as you're told, party hard and eat Kraft Dinner, the most popular meal in Canada, often combined with cut-up hot dogs.

I'm from a place where people care more about doing things for the greater good than doing what's best for themselves; where the land is not littered; where words, not bullets are used to resolve differences; where a good education system helps individuals, businesses and future generations; and where no one gets even sicker worrying about huge medical bills.

I'm from a land where Tim Horton's is a coffee and do-nut shrine, visible on every corner and near every hockey arena.

I'm from generations of family who originated in Scotland and England. I know because "23andme" told me so.

My "Where I'm From" then joined with my husband's "Where I'm From" and as a result, we have doubled the richness of our backgrounds to pass on to our children. It's no longer just about me.

Author Contact Information: djpascoe1716@gmail.com
Cell: 919-740-5644